BUILT TO LAST

Building America's Amazing Bridges, Dams, Tunnels, and Skyscrapers

· GEORGE SULLIVAN ·

SCHOLASTIC NONFICTION

an imprint of

SCHOLASTIC

CONTENTS

INTRODUCTION

From the beginning, *Built to Last* was planned as an unusual and exciting book for young readers. It surely was for me. Investigating how social and cultural advances led to the building of some of the nation's most important structures was challenging and full of discovery. I learned about

- the quirk of nature that led to the construction of the Brooklyn Bridge,
- the enormous robotlike machine that can do the work of fifty tunnel diggers,
- the massive boxlike structure that made it possible for bridge builders to dig foundations underwater,
- the clever fish-startle system used to safeguard the lives of unsuspecting fish during blasting for underwater tunnels.

As you'll discover in these pages, engineers and architects are problem solvers.

Some of their solutions are exciting. For example, magnetic-levitation trains, called maglevs, may fill some of the transportation needs of the future. Magnetic fields suspend and accelerate a vehicle along a track. Magnetic trains are faster—traveling at speeds of up to 270 mph—smoother, and quieter. And they're pollution free.

The problems associated with design and construction will multiply as the world's population increases and environmental issues become more serious. Air and water pollution, energy needs, and the redevelopment of cities are among these problems. The future of design and construction will reflect our concerns for these issues and will, I know, result in bigger and better buildings made with new materials and techniques. What we think of as fantastical today, may be part of the skyline of tomorrow.

© Thayer Burch

GEORGE SULLIVAN

NEW YORK CITY

THE EARLY REPUBLIC
1790—1850

In its earliest days, America was an agricultural nation. Most people farmed and produced much of what they needed. They grew their own food. They cut firewood for fuel. They made soap, candles, and toys for their children.

Beginning in the early 1800s, the nation began to change. Each section of the country started to develop its own character. The North turned to factory production and commerce. The South became tied to cotton produced on plantations by slave labor. In Ohio, Indiana, Illinois, and other parts of the West, commercial family farms were the rule.

The physical links between these regions consisted mainly of crude roads that were used chiefly by people traveling on foot or on horseback. A revolution in transportation soon took place.

To make wagon travel easier between the East and West, Congress provided $7 million in 1811 to construct what was called the National Road. The gravel-topped road went from Cumberland, Maryland, to Wheeling, Virginia (now West Virginia).

People of the day, however, found transporting farm produce or manufactured goods over long distances in horse-drawn wagons to be expensive. They wanted a cheaper way of getting what they produced to market.

Canals were the answer. The Erie Canal, completed in 1825, is the best example. It connected the Great Lakes with the Hudson River and New York City so western grain could be shipped to eastern markets at reasonable rates. And since travel was cheaper and easier, the Erie Canal also boosted the western migration of America's people.

The Erie Canal was so successful that it triggered an era of canal construction. Canal mileage went from 1,300 to 3,300 miles in a single decade. Most of the construction was in western New York. The canal era did not last long, though. By 1850, canals were being abandoned in favor of railroads. Rail lines connected New York City and Chicago as early as 1853. A year later, tracks stretched as far west as the Mississippi River.

The railroads, with their low-cost fares, attracted even more settlers from the East to the cities and towns of the West. The number of farms in the West and the amount of agricultural production kept growing.

The railroads gave western farmers a market in the East for what they grew. Selling their products provided them with cash. Farm families could now buy things. They began purchasing the goods being manufactured in eastern workshops and factories. America was being transformed into a nation of buyers and sellers.

The people of the original thirteen states had little interest in the unmapped wilderness beyond their borders. The Louisiana Purchase of 1803, which nearly doubled the size of the country, changed that. It added an immense new area to the nation and turned people's attention to the western territories. The West offered fertile soil. It meant a chance for a new beginning.

Following the War of 1812, tens of thousands of pioneers set out for the unsettled lands north of the Ohio River, struggling across the Appalachian Mountains, a rugged barricade that stretched from Quebec, Canada, to northern Alabama.

Once settled in the West, farmers realized that the Appalachians barred trade with the East. It took too much time and cost too much money to try to ship flour, apples, and wood over the mountainous wall. The Appalachian Mountains were a barrier for eastern merchants as well. The mountains prevented them from selling their manufactured goods, such as shovels and hoes, hinges and chains, to the West.

A canal, a human-made waterway across the upper fringe of New York State, was the answer. Covering almost 400 miles, it would link Lake Erie in the West with the Hudson River in the East. The canal, carrying barges, freight boats, and other commercial vessels, would provide a safe and easy way to get goods to their markets. It would be called the Erie Canal.

But to many people of the time, the Erie Canal was a foolish idea. How would the more-than-300-mile-long canal be built? The new nation had no experienced engineers who were trained or skilled to do the difficult work. How were the vast forests of great trees to be cut away? How were the tons of earth to be moved? How were rivers, swamps, and hills to be crossed?

Thomas Jefferson voiced the opinion of many, saying the canal was "a little short of madness."

DeWitt Clinton, a powerful New York politician,

LOCATION: Across New York State, between Buffalo and Albany

TOTAL COST: $8 million • CONSTRUCTION DATES: 1817–1825

LENGTH: 363 miles

thought otherwise. He declared that the canal was vital, and not just for New York. Clinton argued that the canal would open up the great American West. It would become the superhighway of young America.

After Clinton became the governor of New York in 1817, he persuaded state lawmakers to provide $7 million for construction of the canal. Engineers were sent for training in England and Holland. Surveyors began to lay out and mark the canal route. The canal was to be 363 miles long, 40 feet wide, and 5 feet deep.

On July 4, 1817, construction began with groundbreaking ceremonies near Rome, New York. Work was divided into different regions along the route. In each region, local laborers did the work with shovels, picks, axes, and horse- or ox-drawn plows and scrapers. They were joined by hundreds of Irish immigrants.

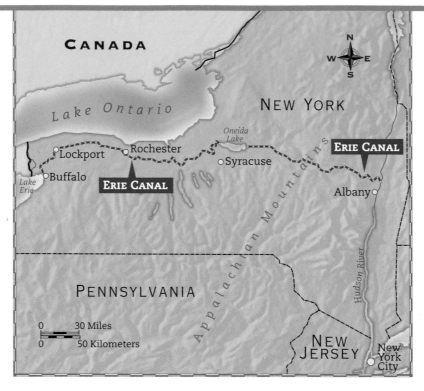

The Erie Canal allowed travel from the Great Lakes, across New York State to Albany, and then south to New York City.

The men cut the trees, pulled up the stumps, and cleared the brush. They shoveled dirt into horse-drawn carts, filled the carts, and then dumped them. And they did it again and again.

They built locks to raise or lower boats and bridge-like structures called aqueducts to carry the canal over rivers and valleys. The Erie Canal required eighteen aqueducts. Raised pathways, or towpaths, were created along the banks of the canal. The mules or horses that hauled the boats walked the towpaths.

After five years of construction involving thousands of workers, people worried that the project was never going to be completed. Newspapers blasted Clinton. The canal was called Clinton's Big Ditch and Clinton's Folly. In 1822, New Yorkers voted Clinton out of office.

The Erie Canal shortened the journey between Buffalo and New York City from twenty days to six days. At the time work began on the 363-mile-long Erie Canal, the longest existing canal in the United States covered less than 28 miles.

But Clinton continued to fight for the canal. In 1824, he was reelected governor. In 1825, after eight years of work, the Erie Canal was completed.

The celebrating lasted ten days. Clinton traveled the length of the canal in a passenger boat named the *Seneca Chief*. Other boats cruised with him. Clinton received cheers and applause at every town.

Within a year after its opening, 2,000 boats, 9,000 horses, and 8,000 men were at work moving goods on the canal. Bullhead freighters carried flour and grain. Square-cornered scows hauled lumber. Sleek packet boats carried both freight and passengers.

Shipments of flour, grain, lumber, and beef went east. Manufactured goods went west. Wilderness towns along the canal were visited by floating churches, libraries, taverns, and showboats.

The canal turned Rochester, New York, into a boomtown. Buffalo and Albany grew rich, too. Since much of the canal trade involved New York City, it became America's biggest and most prosperous seaport.

America's canal era did not last long. During the 1850s, America was seized with railroad "mania." Canals were all but abandoned.

A new day dawned for the Erie Canal during the 1990s. The federal and state government spent millions of dollars to boost recreational use of all of New York State's canals. Small, privately owned sailboats, motor craft, and canoes took the place of barges and freight boats. Cruise and sightseeing boats appeared in greater numbers.

The Erie Canal, a relic from America's distant past, evidence of the nation's boldness, diligence, and vigor, has a future.

GOING UP, GOING DOWN

Locks were essential to the operation of the Erie Canal. They permitted boats to be raised or lowered according to the shape of the land.

Workers built each of the Erie Canal's eighty-two locks out of carefully cut stone blocks. These were held together by a newly invented waterproof cement.

Some of the locks are still operating today. Each takes the form of a watertight chamber, something like a big bathtub. Watertight gates at each end of the lock admit or release the boats.

A boat to be raised enters the lock through one of the gates. After the gate has been closed, water flows into the lock and raises the boat. Once the boat reaches the higher level, the gate swings open and the boat exits. When a boat is to be lowered, it enters a lock already filled with water. The water flows out and carries the boat down.

At Lockport, about 15 miles north of Buffalo, Erie Canal engineers built a series of five double locks, which provided either up or down transport for two different boats at the same time. The only double locks on the canal, they took two years to build. They were completed on June 24, 1825.

Before construction of the Erie Canal, it cost between $90 and $125 to ship a ton of cargo by wagon between Buffalo and New York City; afterward, the cost dropped to $4 a ton. By 1830, the cost of transporting flour on the Erie Canal had fallen to a penny a ton.

To thousands of people from New York State and New England, the thickly wooded Berkshire Hills in western Massachusetts offer exciting fun. There's swimming and fishing and, in the winter, skiing, skating, and snowboarding. Campsites are sprinkled throughout the region.

In earlier times, it was different. The green hills of the Berkshires caused gloom. They rose like a barrier, cutting New England off from easy communication with the rest of the nation.

Farm produce and raw materials from the West could be shipped east only as far as Albany or Troy, New York. Just beyond, the mountain wall presented by the Berkshire Hills put New England out of reach.

It was the same in the other direction. Many cities and towns in Massachusetts were thriving manufacturing centers. But merchants could ship what they made only as far west as the Berkshires.

The solution, a tunnel through the mountains, was first proposed in 1819 and planned as part of a canal system. But with the rapid expansion of railroads in the years that followed, engineers decided to make it a railroad tunnel. They picked Hoosac Mountain, not far from the town of North Adams in the northwest corner of Massachusetts, as the site. The proposed tunnel would allow the free flow of farm products and manufactured goods between New York State and New England.

Before the construction work began, geologists drilled into the mountain to take samples of rock and soil to study. Surveyors established the passage's two entrances, or portals, and laid out the path that the tunnel was to follow.

They decided that the tunnel would have a horseshoe shape, rounded at the top with curved walls. Railroad tracks would be laid on the flat track bottom. Work began in 1851.

Crews drilled into the rock from both the east and west ends of the tunnel, working toward one another. They planned to meet in the middle.

LOCATION: North Adams, MA

TOTAL COST: $20 million ▪ CONSTRUCTION DATES: 1851–1874

LENGTH: 4.75 miles

TUNNEL TERMS

Tunnel workers have a language all their own. Here are some of the special words they use.

ARCH a curved structure that supports weight from above and the sides

CROWN the roof or top of the tunnel

DRIFT the horizontal passageway of a tunnel

DRIFTER the automatic drill that excavates rock from the tunnel face

FACE the wall of rock that is to be drilled

GEOLOGIST a person who specializes in the study of the physical history of the earth

GRADE the upward or downward slope of a tunnel

INVERT the tunnel floor

JUMBO a drilling machine with two or more tiers of drilling platforms

MUCK any debris, such as rock, earth, or mud, to be removed from the tunnel

PORTAL the opening at either end of a tunnel; also called a mouth

SHAFT a vertical passage dug straight down into the tunnel from above through which workers and equipment are moved

TIMBERING braces or supports used to hold up the tunnel roof or walls

At its deepest point, the tunnel would be 1,028 feet below the mountain's summit. It would stretch 4.75 miles, making it the longest railroad tunnel in the world.

Workers were excited by a new tunneling machine that they believed would make digging easier. The machine weighed 70 tons. Its steam-driven revolving steel blades carved out a ring-shaped cut, 24 feet in diameter, in the tunnel's rock face. When it had reached the proper depth, the cavity was filled with gunpowder, then exploded to blast out the center core.

When first used, the monstrous machine's cutters ripped into the rock. A blast of sound echoed through the tunnel. Workers clapped their hands over their ears and choked on the thick cloud of dust.

The machine traveled about 10 feet, cutting a perfect circular groove in the rock. Then it stopped. It could not be started again. The machine was a failure. The tunnel would have to be drilled by hand.

Crews set to work using long, heavy steel drills. They usually worked in pairs. One man held the drill's cutting end tight against the rock. The other, wielding a heavy hammer, pounded away with rhythmic swings. After each swing, the holder slightly rotated the drill.

Once several holes had been punched into the rock, workers filled them with gunpowder. Then they retreated toward the tunnel's opening. A worker bent and lit a fuse. An earsplitting explosion quickly followed. After the dust had settled, muckers, as they were called, moved in to take away the shattered rock.

The work of tunneling never stopped. Eight hundred to nine hundred

In 1874, when the Hoosac Tunnel was completed,

it was the second-longest railway tunnel in the world.

men, mainly Irish immigrants and miners from Cornwall, worked in shifts around the clock. Each shift lasted eight hours.

Despite crews attacking the mountain from both sides, the tunnel advanced at a snail's pace. The best a crew could do was about 10 or 15 feet a week. Engineers figured it would take half a century to complete the tunnel at that pace.

Fortunately, workers were soon able to cast aside the hand drills and replace them with pneumatic drills, which had recently been developed. Powered by steam-generated compressed air, several drills were mounted at different levels on a wheeled platform and rolled into place. The drills attacked multiple parts of the rock face at the same time. Workers were able to drill

Pneumatic drills eventually replaced hand drills; they often broke down, but they never wore out.

deeper holes at a much faster pace.

The use of nitroglycerin instead of gunpowder for blasting marked another advance. Nitroglycerin was more efficient than gunpowder. One pound of the heavy, yellow, oily liquid produced the same explosive power as 15 pounds of gunpowder. But nitroglycerin could be volatile. Scores of workers lost their lives in unexpected explosions.

The long stretches of soft rock and water that tunnelers encountered were even harder to manage than solid rock. Workers said the mixture reminded them of porridge, or English oatmeal. Trying to tunnel through the cereal-like mixture was almost impossible. The walls slid toward the tunnel bottom. The roof caved in on the workers' heads.

It took so long to complete the Hoosac Tunnel—twenty-two years—

that people of the day referred to it as the Great Bore.

The solution was to prop up the tunnel sides and ceiling with heavy timbers. Once the timbers were in place, workers erected walls of brick and brick arches to support the ceiling. The tunnel began to take the form of a long brick tube in places. Some twenty million bricks were used in the tunnel's construction.

Engineers must have sometimes wondered whether Hoosac Mountain was the right choice for the tunnel. It took more than twenty years to build and cost five times more money than originally estimated. Fires, explosions, and collapsing rock took so many lives that some workers began to believe the tunnel was cursed. They called the project the Bloody Pit. Some walked off the job and never returned.

When it opened in 1875, twenty-two years after work had begun, people looked upon the tunnel as one of the great engineering feats of the century. New England was no longer closed off from the West. The direct route through the mountains triggered

In winter's below-freezing temperatures, ice often forms within the tunnel and must be removed.

The Hoosac Tunnel is slightly graded so that the middle is higher than the ends.

This means there is no "light at the end of the tunnel" when looking toward

one entrance from the other. The appearance of light indicates a train is coming.

a business boom on both sides of the Berkshires, unleashing streams of travelers who journeyed east and west.

The Hoosac Tunnel remained the nation's longest railroad tunnel for more than half a century. The 6.2-mile Moffat Tunnel in the Rocky Mountains became the record holder in 1928. Japan's Seikan Tunnel, which opened in 1985, and is 33.5 miles long, is the world's longest railway tunnel today. It connects the Japanese islands of Honshu and Hokkaido. The Hoosac Tunnel still ranks as America's longest railroad tunnel east of the Rockies.

As the twenty-first century began, the Hoosac Tunnel continued to serve as an important link between New England and the West. Each day as many as a dozen freight trains rumble through the dark, damp passage. For the power to endure and serve, the Hoosac Tunnel has few rivals.

Keeping the tunnel in good operating condition is a year-round job. The tunnel's roof needs frequent patching. The signal system undergoes constant testing. Here, near the tunnel's east portal, workers make roadbed repairs.

In 1997, a giant grinding machine scraped an additional 15 feet from the tunnel's roof to enable big automobile carriers and double-stack trains to pass through.

In 1792, when President George Washington approved the original design for the United States Capitol, the city of Washington was a dreary place. It consisted mainly of forests, meadows, and marshlands. Abigail Adams, the wife of John Adams, the second president, found it to be the "very dirtiest Hole," the city's streets "a quagmire after every rain."

The Capitol, however, was not to be located in any woodland or swamp. The building was to be placed on an elevated stretch of land a few miles east of the White House, known as Jenkins Hill. Today it is Capitol Hill.

Washington had a clear idea of what the Capitol should look like. The structure was to be rectangular in shape, with three parts: a large circular hall, or rotunda, which was to be flanked by two wings, one for the Senate, the other for the House of Representatives.

Washington never lived to see the Capitol completed. He died in 1799. Only the Capitol's north wing, for the Senate, was standing at that time.

After Thomas Jefferson became president in 1803, he named Benjamin Henry Latrobe the surveyor of public buildings. The first fully trained architect to work and teach in America, Latrobe foresaw a great domed center between the Capitol's two wings.

But before construction could begin, the War of 1812 erupted. On August 24, 1814, a British raiding party torched the Capitol, the White House, and many other buildings. Only a heavy rainstorm prevented serious damage.

Latrobe resigned in 1817. His dome was never built. Charles Bulfinch, a Bostonian, became the new Capitol architect.

Bulfinch prepared a number of different drawings for the dome and presented them to President James Monroe and his cabinet. They selected the tallest of Bulfinch's several domes. When completed in 1826,

UNITED STATES CAPITOL

LOCATION: Washington, D.C.

CONSTRUCTION DATES: 1793–1865 ▪ HEIGHT OF DOME: 288 feet

DIAMETER OF DOME: 96 feet

CAPITOL CRIME

During the Civil War, Federal troops were housed in the Capitol as construction on the dome continued. At night, men slept on the floors in the Capitol's galleries and lobbies.

Soldiers quartered in the rotunda were noisy and prankish. For entertainment, some slid down ropes attached high on the rotunda's walls.

One day, an employee of the Senate heard loud shouting, pounding, and the sound of splitting wood coming from the Senate chamber. He was stunned to see a number of soldiers breaking up one of the desks with their rifle butts and bayonets.

"Stop! Stop!" he cried. "What are you doing?"

A soldier explained that the desk being attacked was that of Jefferson Davis, the president of the Confederacy. Before the war began, he had served as a U.S. senator from Mississippi.

"We are cutting the traitor's desk to pieces," the soldier said.

The employee explained that the desk was not owned by Jefferson Davis. It belonged to the government of the United States.

"You were sent here to protect government property," he said, "not destroy it!"

Charles Bulfinch's low Capitol dome as it appeared in 1852. Stacked at the sides are the marble and brick that will be used to build the Capitol's House and Senate wings.

Bulfinch's copper-clad wooden dome was the tallest and widest ever built in America. Although a popular success, it did not last long.

During the 1830s and 1840s, the United States grew at a rapid rate. A much larger Capitol building was needed to make room for the senators and representatives from the new states.

Millard Fillmore, the thirteenth president, chose a design that had been

The Statue of Freedom, poised on top of the Capitol dome, is 19.5 feet tall.

It is the figure of a woman wearing tribal headdress.

She holds a sword and shield.

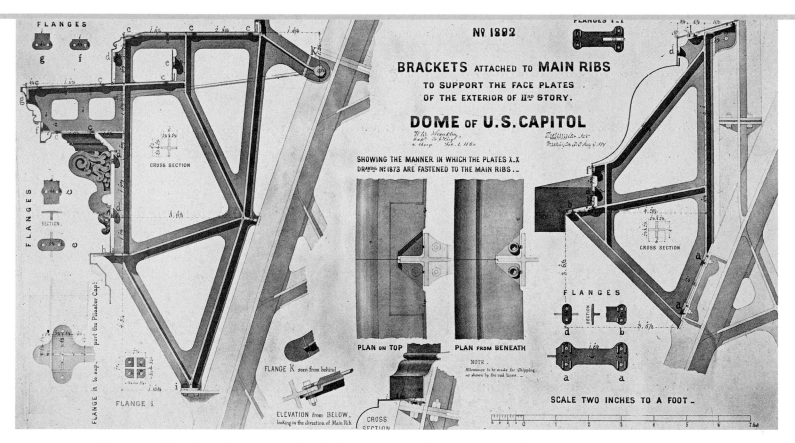

FLANGES

N° 1892

FLANGES I-I

BRACKETS ATTACHED TO MAIN RIBS
TO SUPPORT THE FACE PLATES
OF THE EXTERIOR OF IIND STORY.

DOME OF U.S. CAPITOL

CROSS SECTION

FLANGES

SHOWING THE MANNER IN WHICH THE PLATES X-X
DRAWING N° 1873 ARE FASTENED TO THE MAIN RIBS.

CROSS SECTION

SECTION

FLANGES

SECTION

FLANGE it to support the Pilaster Cap.

FLANGE i

FLANGE K seen from behind

ELEVATION from BELOW.
looking in the direction of Main Rib.

CROSS SECTION

PLAN ON TOP

PLAN FROM BENEATH

NOTE.
Allowance to be made for Chipping,
as shown by the red lines.

SCALE TWO INCHES TO A FOOT.

These architectural drawings detail the form and size of the iron brackets used to support
the dome's columns and faceplates during the additions to the Capitol in the 1860s.

proposed by Thomas U. Walter, a well-known and much respected architect-engineer from Philadelphia.

At the time, Walter was at the peak of his career. He had designed scores of public buildings, including courthouses, churches, and jails. Walter had traveled throughout Europe, examining the great domed cathedrals in Rome and Paris. While he had never been to Russia, he had studied St. Isaac's Cathedral in St. Petersburg, whose dome was constructed of cast iron.

Congress approved Walter's plans in 1855. These called for enormous extensions to the south and north

The Capitol has 540 rooms. However, senators and members

of the House of Representatives occupy space in office buildings

just north and south of the Capitol.

On March 4, 1861, Abraham Lincoln, with outgoing President James Buchanan at his side,
rides up Pennsylvania Avenue toward the unfinished Capitol for his inauguration.

wings and a much more imposing dome. It would be made of cast iron, assuring that it would be fireproof.

Because Walter's dome was much bigger than the existing dome, it required a much larger base. A new and expensive foundation would be needed, Walter thought.

But General Montgomery Meigs, an army engineer with wide experience, had a better idea. He suggested big iron brackets extending outward from the original foundation to support the columns.

Meigs also supervised the interior decorations of the Capitol. He enriched the buildings with sculpture,

Known as the Michelangelo of the Capitol, Constantino Brumidi painted artwork

on the walls and ceilings of the Capitol from 1855 until his death in 1880.

He painted the rotunda's ceiling while lying on his back.

paintings, and elaborate murals.

As Walter's dome began to rise, tensions were building between northern and southern states over the issue of slavery. The Civil War broke out in 1861.

The war transformed Washington, D.C. Many thousands of Federal troops flooded into the city. The grounds of the Washington monument were given over to cattlepens and slaughterhouses. Troops were quartered in the unfinished Capitol.

The war frustrated Walter's efforts to complete construction of the Capitol. Shipments of marble were delayed. Wartime inflation sent costs of materials skyrocketing.

The slowing down of work disappointed President Abraham Lincoln. He saw the dome as a symbol of the nation's courage and determination. Lincoln ordered work on the Capitol to continue.

On December 2, 1863, with the Civil War still raging, the Statue of Freedom was raised to the top of Walter's cast-iron dome. Bands played, and the enormous crowd cheered. By the time the Civil War ended in April 1865, the dome and wings were nearing completion.

In the years since, the Capitol has become the best known of all American buildings. It is famous not only because it is where Congress meets. The building's majestic white dome stands as a symbol of the United States in every corner of the globe.

Constantino Brumidi's painting on the inside of the Capitol dome is almost 5,000 square feet in size and 180 feet above the floor.

In 1899, Congress passed the Height of Buildings Act,

which says that no private building in the city of Washington, D.C.,

can be higher than the Capitol.

ABOUT DOMES

D omes, such as the Capitol dome, have a special place in architectural and engineering history. Essentially, a dome is an arch rotated about a central point, resulting in a shape that is three-dimensional. The weight at the top of the dome is carried equally in all directions toward the base. More than one thousand years ago, the Romans used the concept of the arch to create great domes of stone. Later, domes were a leading feature of Christian churches and Islamic architecture. In the eighteenth and nineteenth centuries in the United States, many civic structures were topped with a dome. You may notice that a great many of the nation's fifty state capitol buildings feature dome architecture. In recent years, many sports arenas have been built as domed structures. Examples include Olympic Stadium in Montreal, and the Georgia Dome in Atlanta. The world's biggest dome, the Millennium Dome, was built in Greenwich, England, to celebrate the start of the new millennium in 2001.

INVENTION AND DISCOVERY
1850—1910

An astonishing number of new machines and processes were invented during the second half of the 1800s. From the beginning of the century up until 1860, 36,000 patents were granted. From 1860 to 1890, the number jumped to 440,000. Among the new inventions were Christopher Sholes's typewriter (1868), Alexander Graham Bell's telephone (1876), and Thomas Edison's incandescent lightbulb (1879).

The American farm saw radical change. Plows had always been horse-drawn, cotton handpicked, butter handchurned, and cows handmilked. After 1860, these and many other tasks became mechanized. To harvest crops, farmers turned to reapers, threshers, binders, and an array of other laborsaving machines.

An important advance came in the late 1850s when an Englishman, Henry Bessemer, and an American, William Kelly, discovered steel, a refined type of iron. Tougher, harder, and stronger than iron, steel led to the creation of vast new industries and brought enormous change to the construction field. The railroads saw notable improvements, thanks to advances in technology.

Steel rails, first laid in 1862, far outlasted the old iron type. They were also safer. Heavier locomotives and new braking systems also contributed to the growth of railroads.

Railroads also benefited from an invention called the swiveling truck. When one of these four-wheeled systems was fitted beneath each end of a locomotive, the train could get around the sharpest corner with ease.

In 1860, there were 30,000 miles of railroad track in the United States. By 1880, total trackage more than tripled, climbing to 93,000 miles. As the nation's chief method of transportation, railroads enabled manufacturers to reach their markets quickly and inexpensively. They also provided easy access to sources of raw materials.

Steel also made for longer, stronger bridges. James Buchanan Eads's three-span arch bridge across the Mississippi River at St. Louis, completed in 1874, was the first structure to make important use of steel. Other steel bridges followed. When engineer John Roebling was designing the Brooklyn Bridge in the late 1860s, he insisted on steel cables.

Heavy steel girders enabled engineers to construct taller buildings. The newly invented electric safety elevator, introduced by Elisha Otis in 1853, also played a role. The upper floors of tall buildings had always been the least desirable because they required a long climb. But Otis's elevator whisked passengers skyward. The upper floors quickly became any tall building's most attractive feature. Thanks to these advances, the new word *skyscraper* was soon firmly fixed in the American language.

For New York City, the winter of 1866–1867 brought bitter cold. The thermometer plunged toward zero each day for weeks. At home and at work, New Yorkers huddled about their fireplaces and wood-burning stoves.

Fierce winds toppled power lines. Drifting snow clogged city streets. The East River between Manhattan and Brooklyn became clogged with great chunks of ice. Since the floating ice kept the ferryboats from running, people in Manhattan and Brooklyn were cut off from one another.

Harper's Weekly joked about the situation. There were passengers who could travel from New York to Albany (a distance of about 120 miles), the magazine noted, and "arrive earlier than those who set out the same morning from their breakfast tables in Brooklyn for their desks in New York."

For decades, a bridge over the East River had been a dream of every New Yorker. The brutal winter of 1866–1867 convinced everyone that the bridge must become a reality.

Engineer and inventor John Roebling had already made several drawings for such a bridge. Roebling had built the Niagara Bridge to span the Niagara River and the Cincinnati–Covington Bridge over the Ohio River. Both were suspension bridges, exactly the type of bridge that Roebling wanted for the East River crossing.

The bridge would consist of two massive stone towers over which four heavy steel cables would be strung. The roadway for wagons and carts and a walkway for pedestrians would hang from the cables.

In June 1869, as Roebling was completing design work on the bridge, he injured his foot in a ferryboat accident. The injury became infected. Within weeks, John Roebling was dead. Colonel Washington Roebling, his thirty-two-year-old son, a bridge builder for the Union Army during the Civil War, took over the project.

Brooklyn Bridge

LOCATION: New York City (over the East River between Manhattan and Brooklyn)

TOTAL COST: $15.1 million • **CONSTRUCTION DATES:** 1870–1883 • **TOWER HEIGHTS:** 276.5 feet

LENGTH, MAIN SPAN: 1,595 feet • **TOTAL LENGTH:** 5,989 feet (1.13 miles)

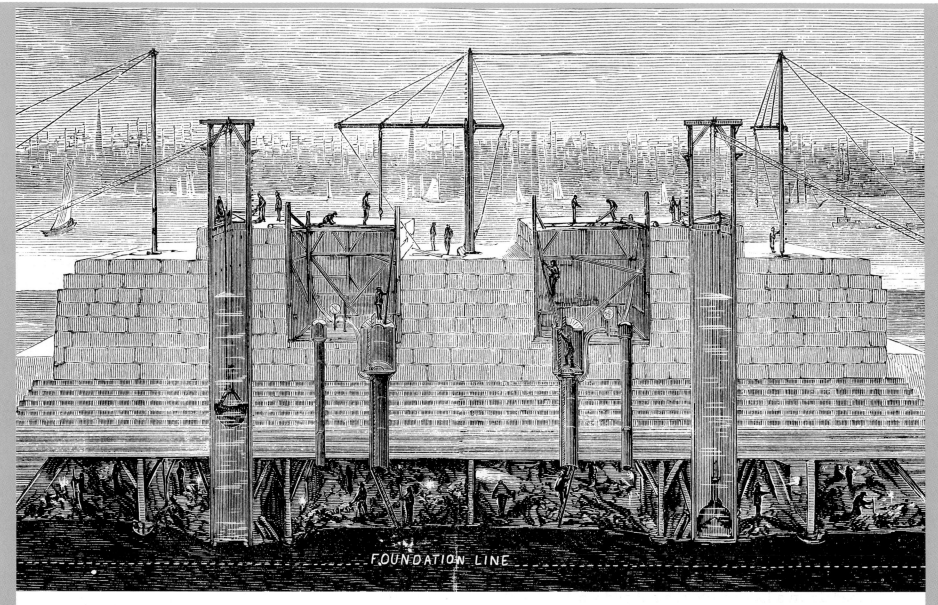

FOUNDATION LINE

This interior view of the caisson on the Brooklyn side of the East River depicts the two shafts (the largest openings) through which excavated soil and rock were hoisted to the surface, the two supply shafts (the narrowest openings), and the air locks through which workers passed going into and out of the work chamber.

On the Brooklyn Bridge's opening day,

150,300 pedestrians and 1,800 vehicles made the crossing.

About 145,000 vehicles now cross the Brooklyn Bridge every day.

Construction work began in 1870. Digging up the mud from the river bottom until bedrock was reached was the most difficult part of the job. The bedrock would provide a solid base for the bridge's two enormous towers.

On a trip to Europe, Colonel Roebling found a clever system for doing the underwater digging. It involved the use of caissons, huge bottomless wooden chambers. Roebling needed two of them, one for each tower.

Each caisson was enormous, about as tall as a three-story house. Built in a Brooklyn shipyard, the caissons were launched like battleships and floated down the East River to where the bridge was to be built. Colonel Roebling rode one of the caissons on its short voyage.

At the bridge site, workers placed big stone blocks on each caisson to sink it to the bottom of the river. Then steam engines pumped high-pressure air into the chamber. The air forced the water out and created a work area between the roof of the caisson and the bottom of the river.

Workers entered the work chamber through iron tubes in the caisson's roof. Each tube contained an air lock where the workers paused while the air pressure was equalized.

Once two or three workers were inside the air lock, the top hatch was closed. A valve was opened to allow compressed air to pour in. When a pressure gauge showed air pressure inside the air lock and inside the work chamber to be the same, the bottom hatch was opened. The men then climbed down a ladder into the hot and smelly chamber to begin work.

Workers in the chamber dug out the river muck while other workers on the caisson's roof laid stone blocks that would eventually form the bridge

INSIDE A CAISSON

Working in a caisson was strange and risky. The air was hot, heavy, and foul-smelling. Light came from flickering torches and candles.

Workers dug away with picks and shovels at the thick muck of the river bottom. They were mostly immigrants. They were paid $2.25 a day, which was good money for the time.

Master mechanic E. J. Farrington described conditions in the caisson work chamber. "Everything wore an unreal, weird appearance," he said. "There was a confused sensation in the head. The voice sounded faint [and] unnatural and it became a great effort to speak."

He told of "the flaming lights, the deep shadows, the confusing noise of hammers, drills, and chains, and the half-naked forms flitting about."

Sometimes the workers toiled in thick muck. Other times the soil beneath the caissons could be as hard as stone. At one stage, crews working on the Brooklyn caisson could dig out only 6 inches a week.

Work crews occasionally came upon huge rocks or boulders. Explosives had to be used to break them up into small fragments.

The Brooklyn Bridge, at 1,595 feet, remained North America's

longest suspension bridge until 1903, the year the

Williamsburg Bridge, also in New York City, surpassed it.

tower. As more and more stone blocks were added, the caisson's bottom edges cut deeper and deeper into the muck at the river's bottom.

As the caisson sunk deeper, water pressure outside it kept increasing. Air pressure inside the chamber had to be increased to keep out the water.

The bridge's four main cables are strung over the tops of the massive towers. Anchorages at either end of the bridge hold the cables in place.

When the chamber reached a depth of about 70 feet, workers inside it began to be struck by a strange disease. A man who had finished his work shift would climb through the air lock and make his way up through the airtight tube to the surface. Within minutes, he suffered fierce pain in his joints and stomach. Workers bent over, doubling up and screaming in agony. Some even died. The disease is known as the bends. It is also called caisson disease.

Many years passed before the cause of caisson disease was discovered. In the high-pressure atmosphere of the caisson work chamber, quantities of nitrogen entered the bloodstream through the lungs. When workers left the caisson for air at normal pressure, the nitrogen expanded into tiny bubbles, causing unbearable pain. Bubbles that blocked the flow of blood to the brain or heart brought death.

Workers were terrified of the disease. Many quit because of it. Today, scuba divers and underwater workers have figured out how to avoid the bends: They must ascend slowly to give their bodies time to adjust to the change in pressure.

In December 1870, fire broke out in one of the caissons. Washington Roebling went down to help fight the

The caisson closest to the Brooklyn shore reached bedrock at 44.6 feet below the surface. The Manhattan tower was a much more hazardous project. There, the bedrock was 78 feet down.

blaze. That evening he suffered an attack of the bends.

Roebling recovered only to endure a second attack that left him paralyzed. But Roebling would not quit. From a bed in his Brooklyn home, he used binoculars to watch and supervise the great stone towers rising.

At the same time the towers were going up, the two enormous concrete anchorages were being built at each end of the bridge. The anchorages would hold the cable ends firmly and prevent them from sagging.

The Roeblings introduced the use of steel for the bridge's four cables. Iron cables, iron chains, and even rope had been used in earlier suspension bridges. But the Roeblings knew that steel was stronger. It enabled longer bridges to be built.

In the summer of 1876, with the bridge's two towers completed, workers began "spinning" the four suspension cables. Each stretched from the Brooklyn anchorage to the Manhattan anchorage, with hanging curves over the two towers.

Cable riggers on sliding platforms began by binding together 278 steel wires, each the size of the wire in a paper clip. Nineteen of these strands (5,560 steel wires) went into each cable.

Each of the four main cables measures 15¾

inches in diameter. Today, they look like thick black lines against the sky.

Once the main cables were up, more than a thousand vertical strands of steel were put in place to hold the roadways and pedestrian walkways. Diagonal steel strands were added for greater strength.

On May 23, 1883, the bridge opened. Stores and schools were closed for the day. President Chester Alan Arthur was among the speakers. Emily Roebling, the wife of Washington Roebling, was given the honor of being the first to ride over the bridge. In her lap, she carried a rooster, a symbol of victory. After the opening ceremonies, anyone who paid the penny toll could cross the bridge.

Through the years, the Brooklyn Bridge adapted easily to change. Horse-drawn carts and carriages were replaced by cars and trucks. Trolley cars gave way to elevated trains and subway cars. In recent years, the bridge roadways have been redesigned to handle six lanes of automobile traffic.

In terms of service, the Brooklyn Bridge has exceeded all expectations. What is considered the nation's most beautiful bridge has proven to be its best designed as well.

In the hours after the terrorist attacks of September 11, 2001, on New York's World Trade Center, tens of thousands of people used the pedestrian walkways of the 118-year-old Brooklyn Bridge as an escape route from Manhattan.

When the twenty-one-story Flatiron Building opened in New York City in 1903, tall buildings were rare. The new structure with its unusual three-sided shape attracted tourists the way the Empire State Building does today. People paid for the thrill of riding the high-speed elevators to the top. From there, they looked out at the busy city.

More than a century later, the Flatiron Building, a symbol of the skyscraper era and a favorite of New Yorkers, still attracts tourists. "The Flatiron Building is special," said a visitor from London. "It's how I imagine New York at the turn of the century. . . . What a wonderful building!"

The most interesting feature of the Flatiron Building is its form. It is located at 23rd Street where Broadway slashes across Fifth Avenue to create a wedge-shaped plot of land. Built to fill that triangle, the Flatiron Building resembles an old-fashioned flatiron, which was used to press clothing.

Because of the building's unusual design, many tenants have to cope with odd-shaped offices. Those at the very front of the building are triangular. Very spacious offices are at the building's rear.

The Flatiron Building was designed by D. H. Burnham & Company, a Chicago architectural firm. Daniel Burnham himself, the company's founder, was a city planner and one of the foremost architects of the nineteenth century.

Burnham was born in Henderson in upstate New York in 1846. His first job as an architectural draftsman was making mechanical drawings for famed Chicago architect William LeBaron Jenny. Burnham left Jenny in 1873 to start his own company.

At the time, the traditional method of construction called for the floors of tall buildings to be supported by thick walls. As buildings got taller, the walls kept getting thicker and thicker. Chicago's sixteen-story Monadnock Building, completed in 1893, was then one of the nation's tallest buildings. It had walls that were 5 feet thick at its base.

LOCATION: New York, NY

TOTAL COST: $22 million • **CONSTRUCTION DATES:** 1901–1903

HEIGHT: 285 feet

Fifth Avenue and Flat Iron Building,
New York City.

GOING UP, GOING DOWN

Elevators were vital in the development of sky-scrapers. Up until the mid-1800s, riding in an eleva-tor was risky. The hoisting ropes sometimes broke, sending platforms or cars on a downward plunge.

A turning point came in 1853, when Elisha Otis invented the safety elevator. It offered a spring mechanism that broke the fall of the elevator if the hoisting ropes failed.

Otis enjoyed demonstrating his elevator by riding up and down in an early model and occa-sionally cutting the rope that lifted it. Onlookers gasped in horror, but Otis's invention quickly halted his descent.

Before the elevator, buildings were seldom more than six stories in height. And no one wanted to climb to the upper floors. But elevators made the upper floors easy to reach.

When the Flatiron Building opened, it had six elevators that were operated by hand levers with-in the cars. Automatic controls were installed in 1960. The system was completely modernized in 2001. At that time, an engineer estimated that the building's elevators, nearly a century old, had traveled one million miles.

By the time the Monadnock Building was completed, the concept of weight-bearing walls in the construction of tall buildings had begun to fade. William LeBaron Jenny, Burnham's early employer, pioneered the change. In his ten-story Home Insurance Building, built in Chicago and completed in 1885, Jenny directed that the floors be supported by a steel skeleton of vertical columns and horizontal beams. The walls were merely the building's skin.

The Home Insurance Building is considered by many to be the first American skyscraper. The building was torn down in 1931.

After the Home Insurance Building went up, one tall steel-frame build-ing after another rose in Chicago. By the 1890s, the craving to build tall buildings had spread to New York.

Daniel Burnham's architectural firm was at the forefront of the build-ing boom. When called upon to design the Flatiron Building in 1902, Burnham's company was on its way to becoming the world's largest archi-tectural firm.

Daniel Burnham did no architectural designing himself, however. He left that to others, while he handled the firm's planning and problem solving. Who did design the Flatiron Building? Drawings in the collection of the Art Institute of Chicago give a clue. They show in great detail how the building took form. The drawings are signed by Frederick P. Dinkelberg, who was a junior partner in Burnham's company. Dinkelberg surely played a bigger role in the actual design of the Flatiron Building than Burnham himself.

The Flatiron Building is sometimes cited as once being

New York City's tallest building, but it never held that title.

The Flatiron Building was one of New York's early steel-framed buildings. Once construction began, spectators gathered daily to watch the frame take shape. As one floor was added to another, some felt the great pile of steel was dangerous. They thought it might topple over in a strong wind. People called it Burnham's Folly.

The structure is clad in a pale building stone known as limestone. A hard-baked clay known as terra-cotta was used in creating the building's rich detailing. Designs include elegant floral patterns and gloomy Greek faces.

The Flatiron Building was built by the George A. Fuller Company. For a time, it was called the Fuller Building. But soon its nickname became popular. Nobody calls it the Fuller Building today.

In recent years, the building has given its name to an entire neighborhood. New York's Flatiron District is a lively business area with many stylish restaurants and shops. The Flatiron Building is a striking centerpiece for the distict.

Once the steel skeleton was in place, layers of limestone and ribbons of windows were added.

After taking pictures of the Flatiron Building on a foggy day, noted photographer Alfred Stieglitz said, "It appeared to be moving toward me like the bow of a monster ocean steamer."

ACHIEVING EXCELLENCE

Daniel Burnham, whose architectural firm was responsible for the Flatiron Building, often drew upon the architecture of ancient Greece and Rome in designing twentieth-century buildings. The Flatiron Building is a good example. Its design is based on a Greek column. Like a column, the building is divided into three parts: a base, a shaft, and an upper portion, or capital. The building's base is made up of the tall windows of the shops on the ground floor. The middle portion of the building, with a dozen windowed floors, all of exactly the same design, resembles the Greek column's long shaft. Above these, ornamental stone forms the building's capital. The Flatiron Building's historic and dramatic architecture makes it a classic.

39

Before 1869, when coast-to-coast rail service became a reality, traveling to the Pacific Coast from the East tested human strength and endurance. The journey from the Missouri River across the vast plains and through the harsh mountains in wagons drawn by horses or oxen was filled with hardship and danger. The Oregon Trail, the most popular route, was littered with the carcasses of horses and cattle and lined with the shallow graves of luckless travelers.

A voyage on a steamship from the Atlantic Coast, around Cape Horn at the tip of South America, then north to San Francisco, was almost as cruel. It was 18,000 miles long. It cost $1,000. Fierce storms made the trip dangerous.

In the early 1800s, people started to talk about a transcontinental railroad. It could shorten the travel time from the East Coast to San Francisco to seven days.

Railroad talk became more serious with the discovery of gold in California in 1848. A great wave of fortune hunters headed west. In 1850, the year California became a state, it had a population of 92,000. Within ten years, it had quadrupled, jumping to 380,000.

Although the population kept growing, California remained undeveloped. There were no foundries to cast iron. There were no factories to make shovels, plows, or wagons. Almost everything that settlers or miners needed had to be carted from the East.

The rich farmlands of the West produced bountiful harvests. Mineral riches lay beneath the ground. But there was no practical way to move western products to eastern markets.

Cries for a rail line kept getting louder and louder. Several routes were considered. When President Abraham Lincoln signed the Pacific Railroad Act of 1862, it settled the matter.

Tracks would be laid between Sacramento, California, and Omaha, Nebraska. From Omaha, the tracks would connect with a rail line to St. Louis and Chicago, and then with a network of existing lines to

TRANSCONTINENTAL RAILROAD

LOCATION: Between Chicago, IL, and Sacramento, CA

CONSTRUCTION DATES: 1863–1869

TOTAL LENGTH: 1,800 miles

Boston, New York, Philadelphia, and Baltimore.

Two companies were assigned to build the new line— the Central Pacific (later named the Southern Pacific) and the Union Pacific. The Central Pacific would begin in Sacramento and lay tracks toward the east. The Union Pacific was to lay tracks in the other direction, heading west from Omaha. No meeting point was chosen.

Congress granted both railroad companies large areas of federal land on which to build. In return, the government could move troops and supplies on the railroads at half the normal cost.

Construction began in 1863. Among the workforce were Chinese and Irish laborers and Civil War veterans.

The route of the transcontinental railroad roughly follows the 42nd parallel, an imaginary east–west line parallel to the equator that marks the latitude.

Some of the Chinese had been recruited from China for the sole purpose of working on the railroad, but most were already living in California.

The laborers worked in teams of twelve to twenty men, one of whom was elected to be the headman. Another laborer was named the cook. The crews worked six days a week, resting on Sunday. At the end of the month, each worker was paid $31.

They leveled the hills and filled in the hollows. When a tunnel had to be cut, they drilled holes into the hard rock, filled them with blasting powder, and set off the charges.

A sheer cliff almost half a mile in height along the North Fork of the American River in northern

It took forty railroad cars filled with material to lay just 1 mile of track.

Each mile of track required 400 sections of rail, each weighing

700 pounds, 2,400 wooden ties, and 4,000 iron spikes.

California presented a tough challenge. A ledge would have to be blasted into the steep rock face to carry the tracks. Engineers thought the task to be almost impossible.

A Chinese foreman had an ingenious solution. He asked that stalks of tall swamp grass be sent from San Francisco. When the reeds arrived, he had them woven into baskets, each big enough to hold a worker.

Workers sat in the baskets, which hung over the sides of the cliff. Using small hand drills, the men bored holes into the rock. After packing the holes with explosives, a worker lit the fuse, then hollered to be pulled out of danger.

Some of the workers died in accidents. No one knows how many because the Central Pacific kept no record of injuries or deaths.

The hazards presented by the rough terrain weren't the Central Pacific's only problem. An incredibly long supply line hindered construction work. Every spike, every length of rail, every locomotive, and every piece of construction equipment had to be shipped from factories in the East around the southern tip of South America. At one time, some thirty-five vessels were involved in the operation.

The Union Pacific, laying track in the opposite direction, did not begin construction work until 1865. Union Pacific workers were young and mostly Irish. Many were ex–Civil War soldiers who had chosen not to return home. A handful were newly freed African Americans. When Union Pacific tracks reached Utah, Mormons, who had settled in the area years before, formed some of the work crews.

Amazingly, the entire rail line was built with only one piece of mechanical

FROM DAWN UNTIL DUSK

For Union Pacific crews laying track across the Nebraska plains, a typical day followed this schedule:

In the morning, men awoke at dawn. They washed in a tin basin, ate breakfast, and then joined their work crews. They shoveled or plowed, placed rails on the wooden ties, spiked the rails down, or attached fishplates, which joined two rails end to end. Two rails were laid down and spiked into place every thirty seconds, one on each side. A measuring rod was used to be certain that the two were exactly 4 feet, $8\frac{1}{2}$ inches apart.

At noon, "Time!" was called. Workers went to the dining cars, where they sat on wooden benches at long tables. They ate heartily. The noonday meal included plenty of coffee; hot soup; fried, boiled, or roasted meat, usually beef; potatoes; and sometimes pie, cake, or canned fruit.

Afterward, the workers rested in their bunks. While some napped, others read, smoked, or sewed buttons. At one o'clock, it was back to work.

As dusk approached, "Time!" was called again. In the bunkhouses after supper, men played cards, smoked, and talked. They also sang songs. Harmonicas often furnished the music.

It took three swings of the sledgehammer to drive in one spike.

Each length of rail required ten spikes. The 1,800 miles from Omaha, Nebraska,

to San Francisco, California, required twenty-one million sledgehammer swings.

This famous photo was taken at the meeting of East and West at Promontory, Utah. The chief engineers, Grenville Dodge (left) of the Union Pacific and Samuel Montague (right) of the Central Pacific, are shaking hands. Cannons boomed and bells rang out across the country in celebration. The gold spike was removed for safekeeping, and souvenir collectors whittled the last tie into tiny chips.

Railroad surveyors of the 1860s did their jobs so well that almost a century later,

when engineers laid out Interstate 80 across the country,

their route ran almost parallel to the first rail line.

equipment—the Union Pacific's steam shovel. Muscle power scooped out the dirt, cut through the ridges, leveled the hills, bridged the creeks, filled in the valleys, and blasted tunnels through the mountains.

At one stage, the workforce was of awesome size, numbering fifteen thousand people on each side. The total number was equal to the population for a city the size of Bangor, Maine, or Eureka, California.

Work on both the eastern and western sides was conducted in three stages. The surveyors went first, placing wooden spikes to mark the route the rail line was to take. They traveled on foot, on horseback, or sometimes in small horse-drawn wagons. They camped in the open.

Behind the surveyors came the grading crews. Working with picks, shovels, wheelbarrows, wheeled carts, and horse- or oxen-drawn scrapers, they readied the ground for the tracks. They also strung telegraph lines. Graders were paid $2 or $3 a day, good wages for the time.

Miles behind the graders, gangs of tracklayers toiled. They put the wooden ties in place, filled dirt in between them, laid the rails, and spiked them down.

Crossing the flat plains, the tracks went down in record time. The pace was about as fast as a man could walk. Building the rail line over California's High Sierra was a far greater challenge. Sometimes work progressed at only 1 or 2 feet a day.

On May 10, 1869, at Promontory, Utah, a little town in the mountains north of the Great Salt Lake, the two construction crews met. California Governor Leland Stanford drove the final gold spike to join the tracks. A telegraph operator tapped out the news to delighted Americans: "The last rail is laid . . . the last spike driven . . . the Pacific Railroad is completed."

The first transcontinental railroad has been called the greatest engineering achievement of the American people in the nineteenth century. It had enormous impact upon the nation. It slashed the time and cost for people traveling across the country. Farm products and manufactured goods could now be moved cheaply from one point to another. Mail that cost dollars per ounce to get from one coast to another now cost pennies.

During the 1870s, thousands of miles of secondary rail lines to feed into the main lines were constructed. These served to link widely separated cities and towns. Like no other project, the transcontinental railroad brought Americans together.

The Pacific Railroad Act of 1862 set the distance

between rails at 4 feet, 8$\frac{1}{2}$ inches.

This standard gauge, as it is called, is still in use today.

HARD TIMES
1920—1940

The 1920s ended with a jolt. In September 1929, stock market prices began to fall. The millions of Americans who had poured their savings into the booming market watched in fear. As prices continued to tumble, their fear turned to panic. On October 19, 1929, the stock market collapsed. The day became known as Black Tuesday.

The worst financial crisis in the nation's history quickly followed. Millions of people were laid off. More than a hundred thousand businesses failed. Five thousand banks closed. Thousands of Americans lost everything they owned.

The hard times called for a bold and determined leader. But President Herbert Hoover was cautious. To turn the economy around, he called upon business leaders not to lay off workers. He asked labor leaders not to seek higher wages for their members. But Hoover's strategy didn't work.

Hoover also called for an increase in the money being spent for public works programs, for structures such as roads, dams, and post offices. But the amount he requested was too little to do much good.

In the fall of 1932, Hoover, a Republican, faced Democrat Franklin D. Roosevelt, the governor of New York State, in the presidential election. Roosevelt won with ease. Roosevelt's inaugural address and his promise of a New Deal inspired Americans. The new president championed an array of public works projects to provide much-needed jobs.

The awesome Fort Peck Dam across the Missouri River in Montana was one of these projects. It breathed new life into a deeply troubled area of the nation.

Construction of the George Washington Bridge in New York City, the nation's longest suspension bridge, and the Supreme Court Building in Washington began to take shape during this period. Both projects were supported by government funds.

Several projects that had been launched before the onset of the Great Depression were completed during the early years of the 1930s. The Empire State Building, the Chrysler Building, and Rockefeller Center were added to New York City's skyline. The dream of the Golden Gate Bridge was fulfilled in San Francisco. Hoover Dam, which harnesses the mighty Colorado River, also dates from this time.

The New Deal and government spending did not have a big impact on the Great Depression. World War II, which began for the United States in 1941, sparked the economic upturn that ended the crisis. But the New Deal at least halted the economy's downhill slide. More important, it established the federal government as the helper and protector of the poor, the elderly, and the unemployed.

Millionaire John J. Raskob had what seemed to be an impossible request for William Lamb, an architect and building designer. Build the tallest building in the world, Raskob said, and do it in less than two years.

The year was 1929. At the time, the Chrysler Building was being constructed in New York City. It would rise to a height of 1,046 feet to capture the title of the world's tallest building. Raskob wanted his building, which was to be called the Empire State Building, to be even taller.

And building it fast was just as important as building it tall. Raskob and his partners decided they wanted a building that would be a money-maker. They wanted a building with plenty of offices that could be rented out to tenants. They wanted a no-frills building that would start turning a profit at the earliest possible moment.

Designer Lamb was practical-minded. He realized how much hard work would be involved if he took on the project. But he was also aware that he was being given a chance to build a truly historic structure. He agreed to do the job.

Lamb worked furiously to design the building. At the same time, his partner Richmond Shreve planned the construction schedule.

At the time, the Waldorf-Astoria Hotel occupied the location on Fifth Avenue at 34th Street where the Empire State Building was to be built. After the hotel was demolished, workers dug down to the bottom layer of rock and then began laying the foundation.

EMPIRE STATE BUILDING

The building's steel frame started going up on March 17, 1930. Long-armed lifting machines, called derricks, hoisted the heavy steel columns into place. Steel beams, known as girders, were inserted between the columns. These stiffened the building's frame.

In buildings today, columns and girders are fastened to one another by steel bolts and welding. In the Empire State Building, steel rivets were used. Each

LOCATION: New York City

TOTAL COST: $41 million ▪ CONSTRUCTION DATES: 1930–1931

HEIGHT: 1,250 feet (102 stories)

EXPERTS

As many as forty gangs of riveters worked on the Empire State Building at one time. The best gangs could drive more than five hundred rivets a day.

Each gang was made up of four highly skilled workers: the heater or passer, the catcher, the bucker up, and the gunman. Together, they performed as skillfully as circus trapeze artists.

The heater tended a forge that held about ten rivets. The forge, a small workshop that resembled a backyard grill, heated the rivets until they glowed red. Using a pair of 3-foot tongs, the heater plucked a rivet from the forge, then tossed it underhand toward the catcher. Throws of 50 to 75 feet were common.

The catcher snagged the rivet in a cone-shaped catching can. Quickly, he reached into the can with a pair of tongs, grabbed the rivet, and plunged it into holes that had been drilled into the lengths of steel to be joined together. The bucker up would support the rivet.

The gunman, using an automatic riveting hammer, pounded the plain end of the rivet into a bolt-shaped head. The hammer's intense rat-a-tat punished workers' eardrums.

A worker known as a gunman wields a compressed air hammer to drive a rivet into steel sections to fasten them together. The Chrysler Building, the tallest building in the world at the time, stands in the background.

The Empire State Building contains ten million bricks, 120 miles of pipe, and more than 1,000 miles of telephone cable.

rivet had a head at one end; the other end was plain.

While the rivet was red-hot, the plain end was thrust into the precut holes of two or more steel beams or girders. The plain end was then hammered into a second head, firmly locking the steel pieces together.

On each floor, workers laid temporary railroad tracks. Small carts ran on the tracks, delivering metal parts, wooden forms, pipes, tubes, and other materials to where they were needed.

Spectators on the ground looked up in awe at the rising steel frame that teemed with steelworkers, bricklayers, carpenters, electricians, plumbers, sheet metal workers, elevator installers, and other tradesmen. At the peak period of construction, more than three thousand workers were on the job at one time. "Like little spiders they toiled, spinning a fabric of steel against the sky," said The New Yorker.

Elevators sped construction workers from the street to their job sites. When some men returned to work late after lunch, the builders decided to install cafeterias in the partially finished building. As the building got taller, more cafeterias were added. Eventually there were five cafeterias, the highest on the 64th floor.

The builders also hired teenage boys to deliver drinking water to the workers on the job. Each boy carried a bucket of water and a long-handled cup called a dipper.

The water boys did not hesitate to venture out onto steel beams at the building's highest levels. "I learned never to look down," said one. "Just look toward the end of the beam."

The building went up at a furious pace, rising at an average rate of four and a half stories a week. In six months, workers had completed the steel frame up to the 86th floor. A 200-foot tower was then added.

The tower was fitted with what was called a mooring mast for docking airships, the huge lighter-than-air crafts that were popular at the time. After being secured to the mast, the airship would take on or off-load passengers. But the idea came to be judged as too risky. The mooring mast was never used as planned.

One year and forty-five days after steelwork began, the building was complete. Shreve and Lamb could rejoice; they had beaten the deadline with ease.

The Empire State Building opened on May 31, 1931. To John Jakob Raskob's delight, it outdid the Chrysler Building by 204 feet.

The Empire State Building has appeared in about ninety movies.

King Kong is the most famous.

Besides being very tall, the Empire State Building is very strong. Its web of massive steel columns and girders, encased in concrete to protect them from fire, provides great interior strength.

"It's a big, hunky building," said Ronnette Riley, an architect with offices in the building.

Indiana limestone and granite enwraps the building's steel frame. The architects picked out shiny aluminum for the vertical panels between windows. The stone and metal help to stabilize the building.

Strong winds present a problem for designers of skyscrapers. Winds can cause such buildings to sway scarily. Some newer, very tall, lightweight buildings,

Workers begin repairing a gaping hole torn in the Empire State Building when an Army Air Corps bomber accidentally crashed into the structure in July 1945.

with their glass walls, are designed to swing back and forth by as much as 2 feet. But the Empire State Building sways only a couple of inches, even in the fiercest wind.

Proof of the building's sturdiness came on July 28, 1945. An Army Air Corps B-25 twin-engine bomber, flying through thick fog, slammed into the 79th floor. The pilot was killed, as were two crew members and eleven people working at their desks. About a dozen other office workers were injured.

The building itself, however, suffered only minor damage. The accident took place on a Saturday. The next Monday morning, the building opened as usual, although it took three

The Empire State Building has seventy-three elevators

that operate in 7 miles of shaft space.

The fastest operate at a speed of 1,400 feet per minute.

months to repair the $500,000 in damage to the 78th and 79th floors.

While John Jakob Raskob got a structurally sound building, he did not get a profitable one. The nation was in the midst of the Great Depression at the time the building was completed. Hundreds of offices went unrented. People called it the Empty State Building.

Not until the mid-1940s did the building begin to make money. By 1950, the Empire State Building was said to be jammed to the rafters and one of the world's most profitable buildings.

The Empire State Building held the distinction of being the world's tallest building for forty-one years, until the completion of the first tower of New York's World Trade Center in 1972. Other buildings now surpass the Empire State Building in height, such as Chicago's Sears Tower, now the tallest building in North America (page 102).

Although it is no longer the nation's tallest building, the Empire State Building is special. It is a symbol of New York City. It is an international landmark. Nearly four million sightseers visit the building every year. It is simply the most famous skyscraper ever built.

To form the building's exterior walls, cranes hoisted precut sections of limestone to each floor.

Since 1978, the New York Road Runners group has held an annual footrace to the top of the Empire State Building. A former New York City fireman won the first race. He ran up the building's eighty-five flights of stairs (1,860 steps) in twelve minutes, thirty-two seconds.

MODEL BUILDING

S ince its opening in 1931, the Empire State Building has been a favorite subject of model builders. People have built Empire State Building models using plaster of Paris, and some have even carved them out of soap. Fourth and fifth graders from a school in Brentwood, England, built a 7-foot, 8-inch model from 3,212 matchboxes. A Tacoma, Washington, man used 135 decks of playing cards to create his replica. During the 1990s, an American toymaker was inspired by the building. His company produced a 902-piece three-dimensional "super challenging" Empire State Building puzzle. Once assembled, it made a model that was 3 feet tall. Several different types of miniature models are available at the souvenir shop in the Empire State Building. A heavy, metal replica serves as a paperweight. A slotted model is a piggy bank. A 9-inch model has a thermometer attached to it. The most expensive replicas are made of sparkling crystal and cost $100.

55

Early in the fall of 1933, with the Great Depression at its peak and one out of every four workers without a job, thousands of Americans left their homes and hurried to northeastern Montana and the tiny, peaceful town of Fort Peck. There, the federal government was beginning work on a 4-mile-long dam across the mighty Missouri River. When completed in 1940, it would be the biggest earth dam in the world.

Floods caused by the Missouri River had ravaged the area for as long as anyone could remember. Fort Peck Dam was needed to bring the river under control.

There was another and equally important reason for the dam—jobs. Fort Peck Dam was part of President Franklin D. Roosevelt's New Deal, his plan of action to provide money, food, and other help to those in need. The New Deal was also meant to spur the struggling economy during the Great Depression.

At the height of the dam's construction in 1936, more than ten thousand workers were on the Fort Peck payroll. They worked around the clock and around the calendar. Christmas was the only holiday on which work stopped.

Laborers, those who worked with picks and shovels and did odd jobs, earned fifty cents an hour. Carpenters, electricians, and other skilled workers received $1.20 an hour.

Families new to the area lived in small and simple homes. They worked hard. Winters brought bitter cold. Summers were brutally hot. But complaints were few. People at Fort Peck had jobs, and that was enough.

Dams are built of earth, rock, or concrete. Fort Peck Dam is an embankment dam. It is a massive mound of soil over a wall of sheet steel.

When engineers began planning Fort Peck Dam, it didn't take them long to realize that material from which the dam could be formed was close by. They would build the dam from the thick muck at the bottom

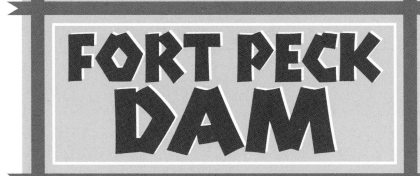

FORT PECK DAM

LOCATION: On the Missouri River in northeastern Montana, 17 miles south of Glasgow

CONSTRUCTION DATES: 1933–1940 ▪ **HEIGHT:** 250 feet

LENGTH: 21,430 feet (4 miles, 310 feet) ▪ **WIDTH AT CREST:** 50 feet

of the Missouri River.

Before work on the dam could begin, workers needed a dry riverbed. That meant shifting the flow of the river around the dam site.

Workers blasted 4-mile-long tunnels out of the rock on the east side of the river. Called diversion tunnels, each was 24 feet in diameter, big enough to hold a two-story house.

Once the tunnels were completed and the river was flowing around the dam site, workers erected a wall of sheet steel across the riverbed. Called a cutoff wall, it would anchor the dam and prevent water from seeping through.

Day and night, tall machines wielding heavy hammers pounded long lengths of steel side by side into the ground to form the wall. The hammers drove each steel section through the ground until it reached the layer of rock beneath the soil.

Fort Peck Lake, with almost 1,600 miles of shoreline, is surrounded by the nation's second-largest wilderness area and wildlife refuge, home to elk, antelope, and bighorn sheep.

"The pounding on the steel was constant," a worker's wife recalled. "All night long it was bangedy-bang. No one could sleep."

With the wall in place, huge dredges mounted on barges began scooping up the watery mix of fine sand and clay from the river bottom. The mixture was pumped through miles of pipes to the dam site.

Once the dam began to take form, engineers made preparations to protect the upstream side of the dam from the river water. Without protection, the swirling water would wash away the earthen dam. Big chunks of rock, called riprap, would solve the problem. A layer of riprap placed on the upstream face of the dam would resist the river's destructive action.

Engineers found the rock they needed at Snake Butte, about 30 miles west of the dam site. Day and

The Fort Peck area is one of the richest fossil sites in the world.

In 1902, it yielded the first skeleton of the *Tyrannosaurus rex*,

the king of the dinosaurs.

night, workers cut, drilled, and blasted rock out of Snake Butte and loaded it onto railroad flatcars for delivery to the dam. Some of the rocks were huge, the size of an SUV and even bigger. They weighed from 2 to 10 tons.

Meanwhile, other work crews continued to pump soil along the length of the dam. Once the water had drained out of the soil and it had dried and hardened, railroad flatcars began dumping riprap on top of the hill of soil that had been formed.

The last load of riprap arrived in October 1940. Fort Peck Lake had already begun forming behind the dam. It grew to be the largest body of water in Montana. It is 132 miles long and 16 miles wide. Its 1,520-mile shoreline is about equal to the length of California's coastline.

In 1943, in the midst of World War II, the federal government ordered the building of a power plant at the dam site. The plant's machinery produced electricity from the power of the river water. Homes and factories as far away as Great Falls, Montana, almost 300 miles to the west, received electricity from the power plant. A second power plant was built at Fort Peck in 1959. Both continue to produce electricity for the area.

In recent years, Fort Peck Lake has come to mean fun and relaxation. Recreation areas surrounding the lake boast paved roads, electricity, showers, picnic tables, and playgrounds for children. The summer brings thousands of vacationers who enjoy camping, boating, fishing, hunting, and sightseeing. Few visitors remember the dam's great importance in providing desperately needed jobs during the bleak years of the Great Depression.

BOOMTOWN

More than a dozen small towns for workers and their families sprang up almost overnight within a few miles of the dam site. They had such names as New Deal, Square Deal, and Delano (which was President Roosevelt's middle name).

Wheeler was another boomtown. It had 3,500 residents. Dozens of businesses lined both sides of the main street. They included grocery stores, drugstores, churches, bars, hotels, and bunkhouses, where some workers slept.

Families lived in crudely built cabins or houses with only one or two rooms. "Wheeler is all wood," a visitor once said. "There isn't a stone or steel building in town." Wheeler had no water system. The people drew their water from wells.

"I remember when people were everywhere, and it was like a beehive," said a one-time resident. "Things never shut down."

Once the dam was completed and there was no more work, people abandoned Wheeler and the other boomtowns. With only one or two exceptions, the old buildings have crumbled away. Towns such as Wheeler exist only in people's memories and old snapshots.

The entire population of the state of Tennessee, about five million people,

could stand on the surface of Fort Peck Dam and not rub shoulders.

California and the Southwest had a problem, a serious one. It was a problem that had existed since Los Angeles was no more than a dusty Mexican pueblo, with cattle grazing on the brown hills. The problem was water.

Water was in short supply. Without water, the land was scarcely fit for cacti and horned lizards.

During the early years of the Great Depression, the problem got worse. When thousands of families in the Midwest lost their farms because they were unable to pay their debts, they traveled to California to seek a better life. Between 1920 and 1940, California's population doubled.

One state official looked upon the vast army of newcomers with alarm. "Not one of them brings any water," he said.

Engineers believed they could solve the water problem. The answer lay with the mighty Colorado River. The brown and silty Colorado began in the Rocky Mountains. It then flowed for more than 1,000 miles through some of the driest land in the Southwest.

To farmers of the region, the Colorado was both a blessing and a curse. In the spring, it often flooded, destroying crops. In the summer's fierce heat, it dried up, and growing plants would shrivel and die.

A dam across the Colorado River would help control the unpredictable flow. Just as important, a power plant built as part of the dam project would provide great quantities of electricity for Nevada, Arizona, and neighboring states.

Engineers had studied the river and selected Boulder Canyon as a site for the dam. About 30 miles southeast of Las Vegas, the granite-walled canyon was rugged and remote. Summer temperatures soared to 120 degrees. No roads existed within miles of Boulder Canyon.

Engineers moved the dam site a short distance downriver to Black Canyon. The river was narrower there, and the canyon walls were higher. Despite the change, everyone still called the project Boulder

HOOVER DAM

LOCATION: Black Canyon on the Colorado River (on the Colorado-Arizona border)

TOTAL COST: $385 million · CONSTRUCTION DATES: 1931–1936

HEIGHT: 726 feet · WIDTH AT CREST: 1,224 feet

To house the thousands of unemployed that flocked to southern Nevada to work on the dam, Boulder City, 33 miles southeast of Las Vegas, was created where once there was only barren desert.

Canyon Dam, or simply Boulder Dam.

President Herbert Hoover often spoke out in favor of the dam. The nation was in the midst of the Great Depression. Millions of people were out of work.

President Hoover knew that building Boulder Dam would create much-needed jobs.

News of the dam was released early in 1931. Thousands of hopeful workers swarmed the area.

When Hoover Dam was completed in 1935, it ranked as the world's highest dam. Today, it is the eighteenth highest.

At the peak period of employment, 5,218 workers toiled at Hoover Dam.

They overran Las Vegas, then a small, sleepy desert town. So engineers built an entirely new town closer to the dam site. The new town was named Boulder City. Dormitories were built for single men. Small cottages for families to live in were put up.

As work began, engineers faced great obstacles. Work on the dam could not begin until the riverbed was dry. The mighty Colorado River had to be temporarily rerouted around the canyon.

Before construction of the dam could begin, four enormous tunnels like this one had to be blasted through the canyon walls to carry the river around the construction site. Today, these tunnels are used to drain water out of the reservoir if it gets too high.

on either side of the canyon. Each was 56 feet in diameter, big enough to hold a five-story building, and almost a mile long.

To create the tunnels, work crews first floated their drilling equipment on barges downstream from where the dam was to be located. They anchored the barges at the work site. To drill, they used a huge motorized rig called a jumbo. It was fitted with thirty heavy steel rock drills. Workers drilled holes in the rock wall, then filled the holes with dynamite and blasted. After a blast, other workers moved in and carted off the rubble. The drilling and blasting went on for almost a year.

Crews of miners set to work blasting tunnels through the canyon's solid rock walls above the dam site. The tunnels would divert the river around the dam site. There were to be four tunnels in all, two

About 4.5 million cubic yards of concrete were poured to make Hoover Dam.

That much concrete could pave a 16-foot-wide highway

from San Francisco to New York City.

DAREDEVILS

During the construction of the dam, huge chunks of rock falling from the towering canyon walls threatened the lives of those working below. Daring workers, known as high-scalers, were hired to remove the loose rock before it fell.

Seated on a short plank that hung from a rope, the high-scaler lowered himself down the face of the canyon. He wore a wide belt that was heavy with tools. Wielding a chattering jackhammer, he chipped away at the rock pieces. He drilled holes in large rocks and placed dynamite in them, then hauled himself to the top of the cliff to await the explosion of the charge.

High-scalers moved about the face of the cliff like circus performers. Tourists who visited the site stared at them in awe.

"I got paid $5.50 a day to start with," one high-scaler recalled. "Afterwards, I got $5.60. I believe that it was one of the safest jobs they had. Less people got hurt high-scaling than on lots of other jobs."

Some high-scalers liked their high-risk jobs because they didn't have to be on their feet all day. "You were sitting down all the time," said one.

When the tunnels were finished and the river was flowing through them, workers began digging out the silt and gravel in the riverbed. They had to dig down to the bedrock, 40 feet below. The bedrock would provide a solid foundation on which to build the dam.

Once the crews reached bedrock, engineers put 3,400 men to work on the dam. It was to be built entirely of concrete. Two giant concrete mixing plants were constructed nearby to provide a never-ending flow of concrete to the site.

Engineers built a tall tower on either side of the canyon. Each was the size of a ten-story building. Heavy steel cables were strung between the two towers. The cables carried huge buckets of concrete to the men below working on the dam. When a section of the dam was finished, the towers were moved.

Construction of the dam was more complicated than merely pouring a great mass of concrete into a wedge-shaped frame. A chemical reaction causes the temperature within fresh concrete to rise. Within the mass of concrete needed for the dam, temperatures could climb as much as 40 degrees. At that rate, it would take fifty years for the concrete to cool and harden.

Engineers had a solution. They poured the concrete in huge blocks, each 5 feet thick. The blocks were stacked on top of one another and linked together like columns of supersize LEGO blocks. There were 230 columns in all. Together the columns would form the dam.

Steel pipes were enclosed within each block of concrete. Once a block

Lake Mead, which formed behind the dam, holds enough water to cover the state of Connecticut with a depth of 10 feet.

was in place, ice-cold water was pumped through the pipes. The water quickly cooled the concrete, allowing it to harden without any cracks.

By the early months of 1935, the dam was nearing completion. President Franklin D. Roosevelt officially opened the dam on September 30, 1935. The tunnels had been closed, and the Colorado River had returned to its original course. A mammoth lake, named Lake Mead, had begun to take shape behind the dam.

At the time the dam opened, it was still known as Boulder Dam. In 1947, the U.S. Congress named it Hoover Dam in honor of President Herbert Hoover. Some people still call it Boulder Dam, however.

Hoover Dam tamed the mighty Colorado River, providing much-needed flood control and a steady flow of water for a million acres of what are now rich farmlands in the Southwest and nearly half a million acres in Mexico.

At the same time, Hoover Dam's power plants furnish low-cost electricity to homes and businesses in Nevada, Arizona, and California.

Hoover Dam stands not only as a landmark feat in construction and engineering; it is a marvel in terms of all it has achieved as well.

The dam was made up of 230 vertical columns that were formed from stacks of interlocking concrete blocks, each 5 feet in height. This photograph shows the wooden framework into which wet concrete has been poured to form the blocks.

According to official records, 112 workers died in the construction of Hoover Dam.

Despite the rumors, no workers were ever buried in the dam's concrete.

During the early decades of the 1900s, Americans began their love affair with the automobile. The number of automobiles being made crossed the one million mark for the first time in 1916. The number doubled and redoubled in the years that followed.

Millions of new motorists cried out for better roads. They wanted new bridges, too. Bridges would provide shorter routes to get people more quickly where they wanted to go.

For generations, people in Northern California had talked about building a bridge that would link San Francisco with Marin County to the north. The bridge would span the Golden Gate, the mile-wide passage of rough water between San Francisco Bay and the Pacific Ocean.

With the growth of automobile traffic, ferryboats that connected San Francisco and the counties to the north had become overcrowded. Sundays were the worst. On Sunday mornings, many San Francisco families would cross into Marin County in their new cars for a day's outing in the country. Everyone seemed to want to return home at the same time. Lines of automobiles that stretched for miles would form at the ferry terminals.

GOLDEN GATE BRIDGE

As early as 1918, the city of San Francisco had ordered a study of what had been chosen as a site for the bridge. Geologists measured the swirling water's depth, studied the tides and currents, and took samples of the bedrock. They announced that building the bridge's foundation would be "impossible" in what was practically the open sea.

Bridge builder Joseph Strauss thought otherwise. Not more than 5 feet, 3 inches tall, Strauss was energetic and ambitious. He was also stubborn.

Born and raised in Cincinnati, Ohio, in 1870, Strauss was an admirer of the Cincinnati–Covington Bridge over the Ohio River between Ohio and Kentucky. It was the first long-span suspension bridge built in America. The bridge was the work of John Roebling, who later designed the Brooklyn Bridge.

LOCATION: Between San Francisco and Sausalito, CA ▪ **TOTAL COST:** $27 million

CONSTRUCTION DATES: 1933–1937 ▪ **TOTAL LENGTH:** 8,981 feet

LENGTH, MAIN SPAN: 4,200 feet ▪ **TOWER HEIGHTS:** 746 feet each

Strauss admired Roebling's ability to get things done and believed he was capable of great things, too.

Strauss had designed a good number of small bridges for highways, but he had never attempted a bridge of the size required to span the Golden Gate. When the San Francisco city engineer asked him to submit a design for the bridge, the ambitious and energetic Strauss jumped at the chance.

While Strauss lined up widespread support for his bridge proposal, there was much opposition to it. Military experts worried that Navy ships entering or leaving the harbor might collide with the piers

Strong rope nets hung beneath the bridge during construction. Any falling worker—it was hoped—would land in a net.

that supported the bridge towers.

Strauss replied that the bridge he planned would offer more than half a mile of open space between the towers. There would be plenty of room for the Navy ships.

Ferryboat companies and operators also strongly opposed the structure. They realized that the bridge would put them out of business. Environmentalists said the bridge and its highways would destroy the natural beauty of Marin County.

Strauss struggled for years to overcome his opponents. Finally, in December 1928, a judge ruled the bridge could be built.

The Golden Gate Bridge's two main cables are the largest bridge cables ever made.

Each one is 7,659 feet in length and contains 27,572 parallel wires.

That's enough wire to circle the globe three times at the equator.

Strauss's plans called for a suspension bridge. But it would be a suspension bridge like no other. Its center span, the distance between the bridge towers, would be four-fifths of a mile long. The George Washington Bridge in New York City, with a center span of 3,500 feet, held the record at the time. The center span of the Golden Gate Bridge would be 700 feet longer.

Work on the bridge began in January 1933. The nation was in the midst of the Great Depression. Men from every part of the country flocked to San Francisco, hungry for jobs. But the bridge construction companies had promised to hire San Francisco workers only. Out-of-towners tried to get jobs by claiming they were San Franciscans. Some bribed apartment owners to lie about where they had been living.

On the job, there could be no laziness. "Eight for eight, or out the gate" was the slogan that guided bosses. Anyone who didn't work hard for a full eight-hour shift would be fired. There were plenty of men waiting for jobs.

Construction on the massive bridge began with workers building the piers from which the steel towers would rise. The pier on the Marin County side of the bridge was built in shallow water. First, workers built a temporary watertight enclosure of sheet steel, called a cofferdam, around the site. The cofferdam provided a dry place to work.

Inside the cofferdam, steam shovels and men with jackhammers dug until they reached the bedrock. Workers then poured hundreds of tons of concrete into the cofferdam. The concrete pier eventually reached the height of a five-story building.

The pier on the San Francisco side of the bridge was more of a challenge.

DAY OF DISASTER

By early 1937, much of the bridge's roadway had been paved. Men began removing the forms over which the concrete pavement had been poured. They worked from wood platforms, called strippers, that hung beneath the roadway.

It was dangerous work. But the men felt safe because they were working above a safety net, similar to the nets used to safeguard the lives of circus high-wire performers.

On the morning of February 17, 1937, workers heard a sharp, explosive sound. One of the strippers had broken free. It began plunging straight down more than 200 feet to the water.

"I felt the stripper give a funny shudder," said Slim Lambert, foreman of the work crew, "then it lurched to one side. I shouted and without waiting I jumped. I landed in the net."

The net was no refuge. It held the 5-ton stripper for only an instant before it ripped apart. Men screamed as the tangled mass hit the water.

On the bridge deck, workers watched in horror as men in the water began to be swept out to sea. Two men were saved. But ten lives were lost in what was the darkest day in the bridge's history.

The Golden Gate Bridge held the record for the longest suspension span until the Verrazano-Narrows Bridge in New York City opened in 1964. It surpassed the Golden Gate Bridge by 60 feet.

It was to be built a quarter of a mile offshore in 60 feet of water. To get to the site, engineers had to build a roadway over the water. Then, working from a barge, they constructed an enormous concrete cofferdam around the work area. The space inside was big enough to hold a football field. Once the cofferdam was in place, workers poured the tons of concrete needed to form the pier.

With the piers completed, work began on the towers. Huge barges delivered the steel sections for the towers to the pier sites. Derricks lifted the sections into place, and they were riveted together. Some 600,000 rivets were used in each of the bridge's two towers.

By 1935, the towers were finally finished. Engineers started spinning the cables from which the bridge roadway would hang.

Work on the bridge was completed on May 26, 1937. The structure was instantly hailed as

Bundled steel rods, used to strengthen concrete, are delivered to the pier at the Marin County side of the bridge. The concrete was made at a nearby mixing plant.

More than one million tons of concrete were used in building

the bridge's anchorages, where the cable ends are secured.

The weight of each anchorage equals that of 17,000 full-grown elephants.

one of the most beautiful bridges in the world. Its tall and stately towers and sweeping cables dazzle the eye.

On May 27, called Pedestrian Day, the bridge opened to people on foot. More than 200,000 people turned out. Each was charged a nickel to stroll across the bridge.

The bridge opened to automobiles the next day. Drivers had to pay a fifty-cent toll.

It was a festive time. Church bells rang. People cheered. Boats and ships sounded their horns and whistles. In Marin County, people danced in the street. Everywhere, fireworks lit the night sky. The next morning,

So many people wanted to walk across the bridge on opening day that the toll collecting machines broke down! Pedestrians simply flipped their nickels into buckets before joining the throng.

squadrons of land-based Navy patrol planes and fighter aircraft launched from aircraft carriers came out of the western sky to soar in a mass flight over the bridge towers. That afternoon, battleships, carriers, cruisers, destroyers, and dozens of other Navy vessels sailed under the bridge and entered into San Francisco Bay.

Joseph Strauss celebrated, too. He received a payment of $1 million as the bridge's chief engineer. He was also given a gold pass. For the rest of his life, he could cross the bridge without paying the toll.

The Golden Gate Bridge is painted a bright reddish orange,

or what is called international orange.

The first paint job required 10,000 gallons of paint.

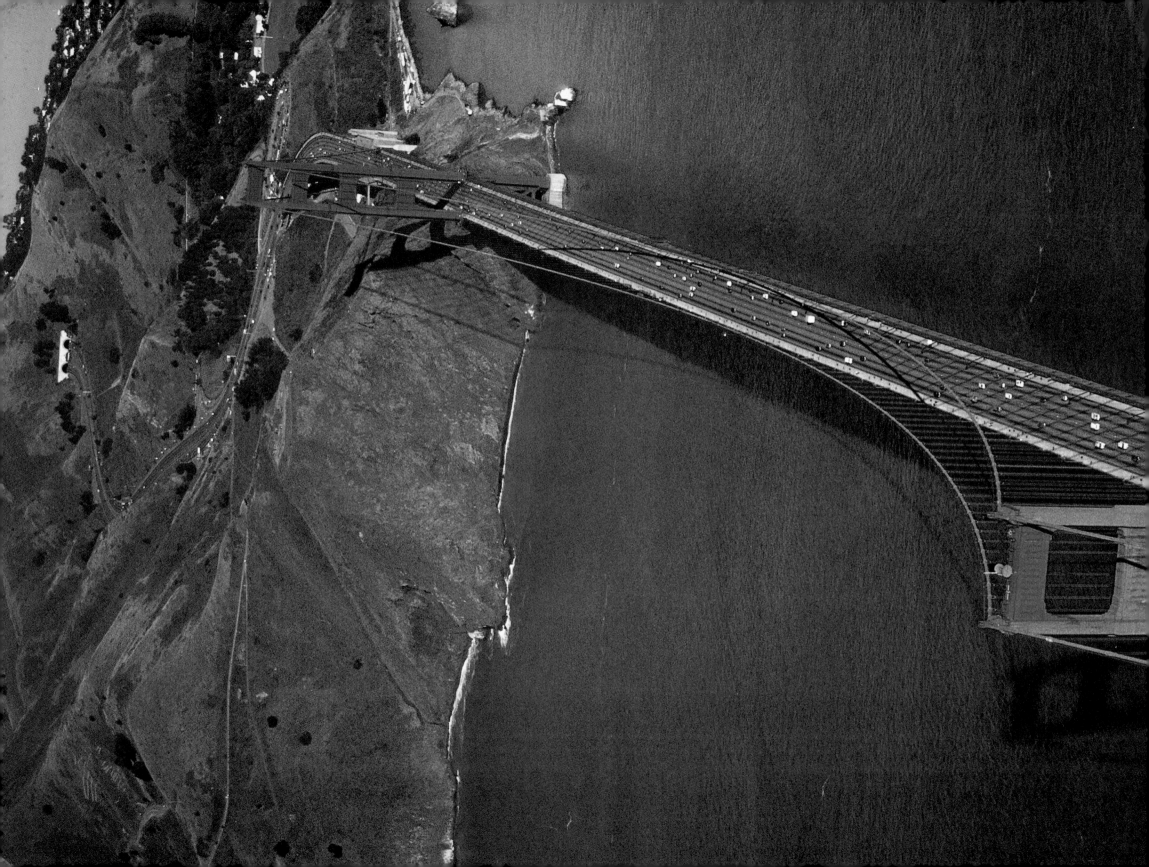

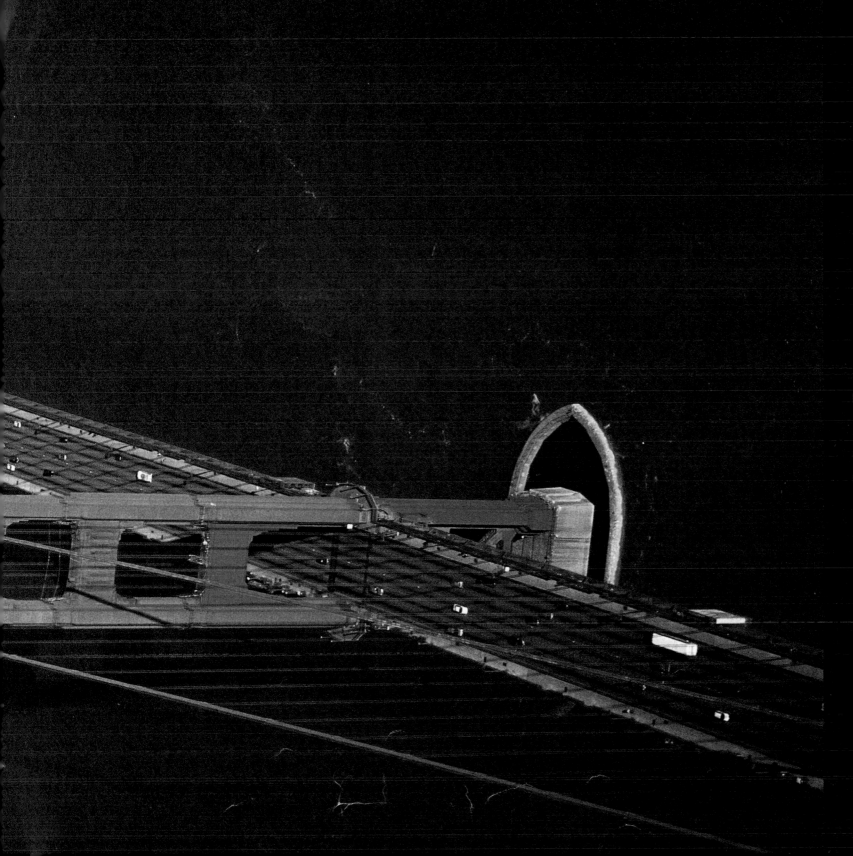

GOLDEN DUD

To mark the completion of the transcontinental railroad at Promontory, Utah, in 1869, a golden spike was used to join the east–west tracks. When the Golden Gate Bridge neared completion in 1931, bridge officials planned a similar ceremony. The bridge would be completed with a golden rivet. The rivet was cast of fine gold from the mines in Sonora, California, and delivered to the site. On the day the steelwork on the bridge was to be completed, the rivet was presented, heated, and inserted in a rivet gun. But when the gunman hammered it in place, the golden rivet broke apart and showered the spectators with red-hot particles of gold. No one had remembered that gold is much softer than steel! Frustrated bridge officials ordered what remained of the prize rivet to be removed. Another rivet was inserted in its place. That final rivet was exactly the same as the bridge's million or so other rivets, made of tough steel from Pottstown, Pennsylvania.

73

Henry White, a paper salesman, awoke suddenly in the sleeping berth of his railroad car on the morning of February 23, 1910. His train had left Spokane, Washington, the evening before bound for Seattle. It traveled west through the hill country of eastern Washington and then up into the rugged Cascade Mountains. But now, just before entering a 2-mile-long tunnel high in the mountains, the seven railroad cars and the big twelve-wheeled locomotive jerked to a stop.

The reason: A monstrous snowslide several miles beyond the tunnel was blocking the tracks. While White and the scores of other passengers fussed and grumbled, plows began attacking the snow.

As the work continued, officials of the Great Northern Railway ordered White's train to make its way through the tunnel to the tiny town of Wellington, just beyond. There was a small hotel in Wellington where the passengers could be fed.

Wellington also offered a railroad siding, a pair of tracks that ran parallel to the main tracks. There, White's train, and a mail train that had also arrived, could be left until the main tracks were clear.

Once White's train was parked, passengers looked out in awe into a yawning canyon below. A towering snow-covered mountain loomed on the other side. "It was some mountain," Henry White was to say later. "You had to throw your head back to see the top of it."

Meanwhile, snow had begun to fall. It kept falling the next day and the day after that. The overworked plows, unable to clear the deepening drifts, began to break down. On the train's sixth night on the mountain, the snow changed to rain. Thunder and lightning, strange for that time of year, pounded the Cascades.

Some time after midnight on March 1, a great

CASCADE TUNNEL

LOCATION: Chelan and King counties, WA

TOTAL COST: $14 million • **CONSTRUCTION DATES:** 1926–1929

LENGTH: 7.79 miles

mass of snow near the top of the mountain broke loose. The avalanche roared down the mountain, gathering everything in its path. It snapped trees as if they were matchsticks. It jarred loose boulders free.

When the avalanche reached Wellington, it never paused but swept the trains to the bottom of the canyon. The cars were so thoroughly buried by snow that it took rescue crews six hours to find them.

Henry White managed to survive with a chest injury. But 101 people died that night in what was America's deadliest avalanche ever.

Years before, officials of the Great Northern Railway had talked of building a tunnel farther down the mountain, where avalanches were less likely to occur. The disaster at Wellington made such a tunnel essential.

Attacking the solid-granite mountain with dynamite and 11-foot drills, work crews cut through the mountain at the rate of 30 to 40 feet a day.

World War I (1917–1918) delayed work on the new tunnel. After the war, engineers mapped out the tunnel's route. It would follow an arrow-straight line through the Cascades between the towns of Scenic and Berne, Washington. Almost 8 miles in length, it would be the longest railroad tunnel on the North American continent.

More than two thousand workers were recruited to join the project. To speed construction, they attacked the mountain from four different sites. One work party, or gang, as it was called, began drilling into the mountain at the east portal. A second gang tackled the west portal. The two crews worked toward each other.

Engineers also drilled straight down above the tunnel line at Mill Creek, about 2 ½ miles from the east

Workers celebrated late in 1928 when men in the east and west sections of the tunnel broke

through the thin wall of rock that separated the two crews. The engineers' calculations were so

precise that the two tunnel headings were only 7 inches out of line.

portal. When diggers reached the level the tunnel was to take, two work crews were lowered into the shaft. Each began drilling outward toward the portals.

At each site, crews worked seven days a week, drilling day and night in eight-hour shifts. They operated drilling machines with four platforms. Each platform supported several 11-foot-long steel drills powered by compressed air. Drillers were able to attack the rock face at four different levels at the same time.

When the drilling was done, workers packed dynamite into the drill holes. Everyone then retreated toward the tunnel entrance, leaving only one worker, known as the shifter, to set off the dynamite.

A huge excavating machine cleared away the loosened rock and dirt and loaded it into wagons. Outside the tunnel, the wagons transferred their loads of debris to big dump trucks, which hauled away the rubble.

The Cascade Tunnel knifes its way through one of the hundreds of sharp rock peaks that make up the Cascade Mountain range. These mountains have heavy snowfall and sizable glaciers. Thick rain forests cover the narrow valleys between the mountains.

Several small towns sprang up for the hundreds of workers who toiled at the tunnel site. Each town had its own hospital, school, and large hall that was used as a library as well as for dances and movies.

PRESIDENTIAL VISIT

Late in April 1928, President Calvin Coolidge traveled to the Cascade Tunnel work site. The president made the trip to set off a blast of dynamite that removed a thin rock barrier to open a pioneer tunnel, which had been hollowed out alongside the main tunnel.

The pioneer tunnel, a temporary tunnel, was much smaller in diameter than the main tunnel. Even so, it took two years to build. A series of passages, known as crosscuts, linked it to the main tunnel.

The pioneer tunnel had many uses. Pipes ran through it, bringing compressed air to the rock drills. It carried the electrical power lines that lit the main tunnel. The pioneer tunnel also helped provide fresh air to the workers in the main tunnel.

Workers installed a small rail line in the pioneer tunnel, too. Railcars delivered supplies and men to tunnel work sites.

Using the pioneer tunnel helped speed work on the main tunnel by keeping it free of clutter. This plan was the chief reason that the main tunnel was completed in record time. The president's visit was most appropriate.

After a train has completed its trip through the tunnel, a metal door drops to seal the opening and allow powerful fans to draw out the diesel fumes.

After the deadly avalanche of March 1, 1910, officials of the

Great Northern Railway, eager to erase memories of the tragedy,

changed the name of the station at Wellington from Wellington to Tye.

As the main tunnel got longer, other work crews began lining the walls of the tunnel with a watertight layer of concrete that was 2 feet thick. Portable cement mixers kept the crews supplied with concrete.

On January 12, 1929, the Cascade Tunnel was officially dedicated, and the first train passed through it. Almost 8 miles of blasting and digging had been completed within three years, a record-breaking effort. The Cascade Tunnel made all other tunnel building feats up to that time seem much less awesome.

Today, trains of the Burlington Northern Santa Fe Railway (formerly the Great Northern Railway) whisk through the tunnel in a matter of minutes. They carry business travelers and vacationers between the Pacific Coast and eastern Washington, Idaho, North Dakota, and the upper Midwest. Few passengers realize that the Cascade Tunnel was looked upon as one of the truly amazing engineering feats of its day. Fewer still are aware of the terrible disaster that led to its construction.

Both passenger and freight trains use the Cascade Tunnel today. Freight trains carry many things, including cars, coal, and grain.

Workers installed a new ventilation system to bring fresh air into the Cascade Tunnel in 1956. It allowed diesel engines to use the tunnel.

A GOLDEN AGE
1950—1965

The 1950s and early 1960s in America were a time of optimism and confidence. People felt good about themselves.

The booming economy was one reason for the self-satisfaction. The automobile industry was enjoying the greatest surge of growth in its history. More than fifty-two million automobiles traveled American highways in 1952, an increase from twenty-five million in 1945. The rapid expansion of the suburbs kept increasing the demand for new homes. TV sets, stereos, dishwashers, and garbage disposals were new products Americans felt they had to have.

Advances in production techniques helped spur the nation's growth. Electronic computers, which first became widely available in the mid-1950s, sped up work in factories and offices. What was called the baby boom, an upswing in the nation's birth rate, was a factor, too. During the 1950s, the nation's population jumped by 20 percent.

The passage of the Interstate Highway Act in 1956 contributed to the nation's growth and prosperity. It provided more than $100 billion over the next two decades for inter-

state highway construction. The legislation created thousands of new jobs and aided the automobile, trucking, concrete, and asphalt industries.

Not every family had a house on easy street, however. Some thirty million Americans continued to live in poverty. And the 10 percent of the population who were African Americans, as well as other minorities, continued to feel the pain of social and economic bias.

The booming economy and feelings of prosperity inspired American architects and engineers of the 1950s and 1960s. They thought in bold terms and built structures that were bigger, longer, and taller.

The Chesapeake Bay Bridge-Tunnel, a 20-mile-long mingling of bridges, tunnels, human-made islands, and elevated highways became the world's largest complex of its type. Construction began in 1960. St. Louis's Gateway Arch, the nation's tallest monument, started going up in 1961.

The nation's longest suspension bridge, the Verrazano-Narrows Bridge in New York City, and the nation's highest earth-filled dam, the Oroville Dam on California's Feather River, date from this period. Sears, Roebuck and Company began planning a new headquarters in the 1960s. The Sears Tower, the nation's tallest skyscraper, was the result.

By 1960, the American people had achieved the highest standard of living of any society in the history of the world. Today, the nation is dotted with many visual reminders of that comfortable time.

t's the biggest earthmoving project the world has ever known. It has moved 42 billion cubic feet of earth, enough to bury the state of Connecticut knee-deep in dirt. It has used enough concrete to build six sidewalks to the moon.

It has recruited the nation's best engineering talent and used the latest construction techniques. It has cost more than $100 billion so far, and the total cost is nowhere in sight.

It's the nation's interstate highway system, or to use its full name, the Dwight D. Eisenhower System of Interstate and Defense Highways.

Launched in 1956 by the Federal Highway Act, the interstate highway system is made up of sixty-two superhighways that cover 42,795 miles. They link together the nation's coasts and borders, cities, and towns. These superhighways include 54,663 bridges and 104 tunnels.

Throughout the decades, the interstate highway system has changed the landscape of America. It has also brought about great cultural changes.

At the beginning of the twentieth century, automobiles were rare. For long trips, people took trains. For short journeys, there was the horse and buggy. In big cities, people rode electrically powered trolley cars, also called streetcars.

Change came when automobiles began to be produced in large quantities. Car prices dropped as a result. More than a million cars were produced for the first time in 1916. The number grew to four million by 1923.

Motorists of the time called for more and better roads. To satisfy the demand, private organizations, such as the American Automobile Association, were formed. These organizations mapped out their own routes and gave them distinctive names. The New England Highway System, for example, served the New England states and New York. The Dixie Highway began in Florida and reached as far north as Ontario, Canada.

U.S. INTERSTATE HIGHWAY SYSTEM

LOCATION: Throughout the United States

TOTAL COST: $100 billion plus ▪ CONSTRUCTION DATES: 1956–Present

TOTAL LENGTH: 42,795 miles

By 1925, there were more than 250 named highways. They were usually blacktopped and two lanes wide.

Each of the named highways had its own system of signs and symbols. Directional signs were placed on a hit-or-miss basis. Sometimes they were located by the side of the road. Other times they were mounted on bridges or utility poles. Motorists were often bewildered as a result.

The federal government stepped in to end the confusion in 1925, setting up a system of U.S. highways. The named highways were given route numbers and identified with shield-shaped signs.

Concrete, made from cement, sand, water, and gravel or crushed stone, goes from mixing plants to heavy trucks for delivery to highway construction sites.

The federal government also made improvements in road construction. But during the Great Depression, which began in 1929 and lasted well into the 1930s, and during World War II (1941–1945), few roads were built.

There was no civilian production of automobiles during World War II, either. Car manufacturers turned out tanks, guns, and other weapons.

By the time the war ended, Americans craved new cars. When they became available, people snatched them up. More than fifty million automobiles were operating on American highways in the early 1950s.

Those highways were mostly the old U.S. high-

The interstates represent more than 1 percent of the nation's highway system,

yet they carry nearly one quarter—23 percent—of all roadway traffic.

ways, some of which dated to the 1920s. Dwight D. Eisenhower, who became president in 1953, saw the need for change.

During World War II, Eisenhower, an American general, had been supreme commander of the Allied forces in Europe. He was impressed by Germany's system of expressways, called the autobahn. Built in the mid-1930s, it enabled the German army to move troops to different parts of the country with great speed.

As president, Eisenhower worked for legislation that would improve America's highway network. His efforts resulted in the Federal Highway Act of 1956. The legislation provided the money to construct a 41,000-mile interstate highway system connecting all the nation's major cities. The project took decades to complete. Highway upkeep, repair, and construction continue to this day.

The legislation also set rigid standards. Highways were to be at least two lanes wide in each direction. A median strip dividing the highway—often a grassy area with shrubs and trees—had to be included. There were to be no traffic lights, intersecting roadways, railroad crossings, steep hills, or sharp curves.

Red, white, and blue shields, which feature the word *Interstate* and give the route number, identify interstate highways. East–west routes have even numbers; north–south routes, odd numbers.

Roadside posts that mark distances at one-mile intervals are another feature of the interstates. These mileposts begin at each highway's most westerly or southerly point.

LONGEST EAST–WEST INTERSTATE ROUTES

I-90 Boston, MA, to Seattle, WA ▶ 3,020 miles

I-80 Teaneck, NJ, to San Francisco, CA ▶ 2,899 miles

I-40 Wilmington, NC, to Barstow, CA ▶ 2,555 miles

I-10 Jacksonville, FL, to Los Angeles, CA ▶ 2,460 miles

I-70 Baltimore, MD, to Cove Fort, UT ▶ 2,153 miles

LONGEST NORTH–SOUTH INTERSTATE ROUTES

I-95 Houlton, ME, to Miami, FL ▶ 1,919 miles

I-75 Sault Ste. Marie, MI, to Miami, FL ▶ 1,786 miles

I-35 Duluth, MI, to Laredo, TX ▶ 1,568 miles

I-15 Sweetgrass, MT, to San Diego, CA ▶ 1,433 miles

I-5 Blaine, WA, to San Diego, CA ▶ 1,381 miles

I-55 Chicago, IL, to New Orleans, LA ▶ 964 miles

I-65 Gary, IN, to Mobile, AL ▶ 887 miles

Texas is the state with the most interstate mileage.

Its seventeen interstate routes cover 3,233 miles.

An interstate highway ascends a gentle slope near Cape Carteret in eastern North Carolina. Taxes on tires, new trucks, trailers, buses, and gasoline and other fuels, help pay for the interstate system.

In the construction of the interstate system, many of the nation's old U.S. highways were paved over to be transformed into modern superhighways. Others were simply bypassed and allowed to remain virtually unchanged.

The interstates transformed the nation. Americans moved by the millions out of their city neighborhoods to the suburbs. They began commuting to their city jobs.

Stores and businesses shifted to the suburbs, too. When they joined together in a large complex, the result was called a mall. By the twenty-first century,

When the interstate system started in 1956, there were only forty-eight states.

Hawaii and Alaska entered the Union in 1959. Today, Hawaii has 55 miles of interstates.

Alaska is the only state without a mile of interstate.

the "malling" of America was about complete.

Now that people lived and shopped in the suburbs, the next step was to move jobs there. That change led to the creation of edge cities. These are areas on the outskirts of major cities that offer nearly everything the old downtowns once did—tall office buildings, shopping malls, hotels, schools, and movies and other forms of entertainment, plus a great deal of parking space.

Edge cities thrive on the interstates. Tysons Corner in Fairfax County, Virginia, is one example of an edge city. In the 1950s, it was a quiet residential suburb. Being close to Interstate 495, the Capital Beltway that encircles Washington, D.C., helped Tysons Corner blossom into a distinctive commercial area of notable size. Like other edge cities, Tysons Corner has more jobs than bedrooms.

Other edge cities include Irvine, California; Plano, Texas; Edison, New Jersey; and Schaumburg, Illinois.

The interstate highways have also created problems. The flight of people, businesses, and jobs to the suburbs caused distress in the cities people left behind. Cities in the Northeast and Midwest suffered the most. Unemployment increased. Tax revenues plunged. Poor schools and rampant street crime were often the result.

The Interstate Highway System continues to be a powerful force. Congress approves tens of billions of dollars for highway construction each year. Commuter and long-haul railroads receive tiny amounts by comparison.

Some travelers are critical of the interstates. They're cold and impersonal, they say. They're miles and miles of concrete, other cars, and little else. They're boring.

Travel the back roads, say the critics. See farms, homes, and people. Sample local food. Ride down the main streets of Boonton, New Jersey, or Cheyenne, Wyoming.

But be sure to bring a good road map if you're traveling the back roads. Road signs aren't always clear and understandable. You may come upon a detour or two. And there are stop signs, traffic lights, and traffic jams.

A vast majority of American motorists agree—for any serious road trip, the interstates are the way to go.

When traveling an interstate, don't look for billboards. All forms of advertising were banned from the interstates as part of a mid-1960s beautification program made famous by Lady Bird Johnson, the wife of President Lyndon Johnson.

From the time the nation's earliest travelers sought to make their way north or south along the Atlantic Coast, the 200-mile-long inlet that is Chesapeake Bay loomed as a serious obstacle.

Trying to go around the Bay added hours to one's trip. As early as 1705, small boats, known as packet boats, began carrying passengers, mail, and freight across the 17-mile strip of water at the entrance to the Bay.

But boats were not the final answer. In the early 1900s, automobile travel became popular, and the ferryboat service was overwhelmed. Long lines of vehicles often formed at boat ticket booths. Motorists seethed at the delays.

Worse, the ferryboats weren't dependable. In times of thick fog or when heavy storms blew in off the Atlantic, the ferryboats did not operate at all.

Everyone knew that the solution was to build a bridge or tunnel.

But it wasn't that simple. And the U.S. Navy didn't want a bridge. Norfolk, Virginia, just west of where the bridge was to be built, was home to the Navy's Atlantic Fleet. In the event of war, the Navy feared that enemy aircraft would bomb the bridge. The wreckage would plug the shipping channel, trapping the fleet inside the harbor.

A tunnel was no solution, either. Tunnels are very expensive to build. At the time, the longest automobile tunnel in the United States—the Holland Tunnel in New York—was less than 2 miles in length. A 20-mile-long tunnel would be far too expensive.

Engineers spent years studying the problem. Finally, they figured it out. They would build both: bridges and tunnels. The project's two tunnels, each about 1 mile long, would lie beneath the main shipping channels. The Navy's ships would be able to glide over the tunnels with ease. Long over-the-water highways would also be part of the mix.

LOCATION: Between Norfolk and Virginia Beach, VA, and the Delmarva Peninsula on Virginia's Eastern Shore ▪ **TOTAL COST:** $450 million ▪ **CONSTRUCTION DATES:** 1960–1964; 1995–1999

LENGTH: 17.6 miles, shore to shore (23 miles, including approach roads)

TUNNEL MAKING

The two tunnels in the Bridge-Tunnel complex were assembled from massive steel and concrete tube sections. Nineteen tubes were required for one of the tunnels; eighteen for the other. Each tube was enormous—as long as a football field, as wide as two city streets, and twice the height of a railroad boxcar.

One by one, the tubes were slung between huge barges and towed out into the bay. Once in position, each was lowered into the mile-long trench that had been scooped out at the bay bottom. A master diver guided each tube on its descent. Standing on the top of the tube as it slid beneath the surface, he spoke by radiophone to the men above. "Okay, hold it. Now down. Another inch. . . . Easy now. Down again. Hold it!"

Then would come a cry of delight. "Okay! We've got it!" That meant the steel pins from the tube being lowered had slid into the slot holes of the tube already in place.

During one summer, divers managed to lay three tubes in one eight-day period. But during the winter, with its angry storms, months could pass without a single tube being installed.

The Chesapeake Bay Bridge-Tunnel is the result. It is a 17-mile-long chain of tunnels, bridges, and human-made islands that spans the open ocean at the entrance to Chesapeake Bay. The complex is the only direct link between the Norfolk–Virginia Beach area of Virginia and the state's Eastern Shore.

Some motorists refer to Chesapeake Bay Bridge-Tunnel as the nation's longest shortcut. It may well be. Take away the Bridge-Tunnel and motorists have an extra 95 miles, two or three hours, added to their journey.

The Bridge-Tunnel is not merely a remarkable time-saver. It has also been hailed as a marvel of engineering design. In 1965, the American Society of Civil Engineers cited the Bridge-Tunnel complex as one of the world's seven engineering wonders. In making their decision, judges reviewed more than a hundred different engineering projects. These included bridges and highways, tunnels and canals, dams and railroads, and tall buildings.

The winning choices were based on two features: size and usefulness.

When it comes to size, the Bridge-Tunnel complex stands apart. At 17.6 miles, it is the longest complex of its type on the planet. As originally built, it consisted of four human-made islands, two 1-mile tunnels, 12 miles of roadway atop stiltlike supports, two high-level bridges, and 2 miles of raised roadways, or causeways.

In terms of usefulness, the Bridge-Tunnel is also exceptional. Each year some three and a half million vehicles travel the span.

In the late 1960s, the Bridge-Tunnel began taking shape. The project was

The engineers' shopping list for the Bridge-Tunnel was like no other:

4 million cubic yards of sand, 100 million pounds of steel, 34,000 carloads of rock,

and nearly 5.5 million white ceramic tiles to line the tunnel interiors.

so huge that five construction companies were needed. Hundreds of subcontractors and suppliers worked under them. Organizing a sea-going fleet of construction equipment was one of the first tasks.

Enormous amounts of concrete were needed for the project. Contractors built a concrete casting plant at Cape Charles on Virginia's Eastern Shore. The plant turned out huge concrete slabs to form the roadways.

The plant also cast the concrete piles that would be hammered into the ocean floor to hold up the highway. More than 2,500 of these cylinder-shaped castings were needed. Some were as long as 172 feet.

After each pile was pounded into the ocean's muddy bottom, its hollow center was filled with rein-

A ship from the Navy's Norfolk, Virginia, naval base glides easily between a pair of the Bridge-Tunnel's human-made islands.

forcing steel and then sand. Sand was chosen because it would help absorb the impact should a pile be struck by a small boat or, in winter, a big chunk of ice.

Once the rows of piles were in place, a huge crane arrived on the scene. The crane lifted heavy concrete slabs from a barge and placed them on top of the piles. Little by little, a two-lane highway began to take form. At first, it was just a stub of concrete jutting out into the water. Day by day, it got longer. Before a year had passed, the highway led far out into the open ocean, stretching as far as the eye could see.

While one crew was putting together the roadways, another was installing the two mile-long tunnels. For each tunnel, a floating dredge first scooped out a deep

Each of the Bridge-Tunnel's four human-made islands has a surface area of 5 acres. That's about the same amount of land covered by the average major league ballpark.

The Bridge-Tunnel was expanded from one crossing to two in 1999. The added lanes provided swifter and safer travel and allowed for major repair projects without closing the span.

trench at the bottom of the bay. A series of tubes, each about as long as a football field, were then laid end to end in the trench, like a pipeline.

Watertight walls sealed both ends of each tube. Once several tubes were in place, workers entered the tubes and cut away the sealed ends. Tube by tube, the tunnel took shape.

To connect the tunnels on the ocean floor with the over-the-water highways, engineers built four islands, one at each end of both tunnels. At each island, the

Fishermen are invited to cast their lines into the ocean from the Bridge-Tunnel's 625-foot fishing pier. The fish caught include bluefish, croaker, trout, flounder, and even shark.

roadway quickly dips down to meet the tunnel's entrance.

The Bridge-Tunnel opened in 1964. It was immediately popular. Engineers soon began planning an expansion. They mapped out a second set of roadways and bridges that run parallel to the earlier crossing and use the existing tunnels and islands. Construction work on the new crossing began in 1995. It opened for traffic on April 19, 1999.

The 17.6-mile journey over the bridges, through the tunnels, and across the long stretches of raised highway is an exciting and unusual experience. Besides the sweeping views of Chesapeake Bay, you see fishing boats and often a huge Navy ship or two.

At one section, the highway makes a series of gentle curves, and you lose sight of the mainland. Motorists realize that they're crossing open ocean. There's sea and sky and nothing else. In bad weather, the trip becomes a real adventure. Nasty winds whip up the ocean water. They splash the low-level roadway and drench your car with saltwater spray.

It takes about twenty-five minutes to make the complete 20-mile crossing. Most people who have made the trip agree on one thing: It ends too soon.

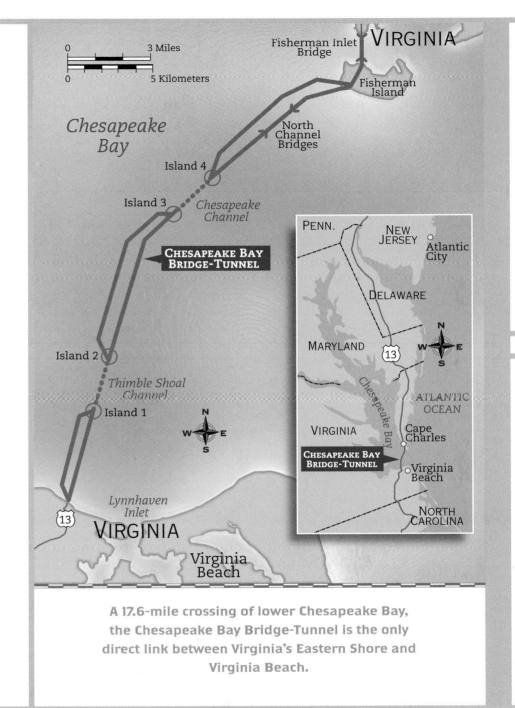

A 17.6-mile crossing of lower Chesapeake Bay, the Chesapeake Bay Bridge-Tunnel is the only direct link between Virginia's Eastern Shore and Virginia Beach.

Almost from the day the city was founded in 1764, St. Louis, Missouri, served as the nation's stepping-stone to the West. Trappers, traders, and members of military expeditions gathered their equipment and supplies in St. Louis, then set out from the city into the wilderness beyond.

During the 1930s, when the National Park Service was seeking a site for a national monument to celebrate the western expansion of America, St. Louis was the choice. The memorial also honored President Thomas Jefferson, who sponsored the famous Lewis and Clark expedition. It was from St. Charles, Missouri, just north of the city, that Lewis and Clark embarked on their remarkable journey of exploration.

In 1935, St. Louis set aside a strip of land along the banks of the Mississippi River as a site for the monument. World War II (1941–1945) caused work on the project to halt.

After the war, a group of civic-minded St. Louis citizens announced a contest to find a suitable design for the memorial. Architects from across the country were invited to submit plans and sketches.

When thirty-seven-year-old Eero Saarinen, an architect who was beginning to be recognized for his imaginative ideas, heard of the contest, he decided to enter it.

Eero Saarinen was the son of Eliel Saarinen, a well-known and respected Finnish architect. Eero's mother, Loja, was a talented weaver, sculptor, and photographer.

The Saarinens moved to the United States from Finland in 1923, when Eero was thirteen. He studied architecture at Yale University and later in Europe. Afterward, he became his father's partner in the family architectural firm. Eero and his father worked together on many different projects. In 1947, when Eero entered the contest to find a designer for the Jefferson National Expansion Memorial, he saw it as a chance to do something on his own.

But Eero Saarinen did not want to design some-

JEFFERSON NATIONAL EXPANSION MEMORIAL ARCH

LOCATION: St. Louis, MO

TOTAL COST: $30 million • CONSTRUCTION DATES: 1961–1965

HEIGHT: 630 feet • DISTANCE BETWEEN LEGS AT GROUND LEVEL: 630 feet

As the arch neared completion, a long stabilizing strut was raised into place to brace the legs. It was removed once the two legs were joined.

thing that had been done before. His monument would not be a dome; it would not be a rectangular box or shaft of stone. Saarinen's goal, as he put it, was "to create a monument that would have lasting significance and be a landmark for our time."

Saarinen won the contest and achieved his goal. He designed a soaring stainless steel arch that rises majestically from its site alongside the Mississippi River. At a height of 630 feet, it is the nation's tallest monument, 75 feet taller than the Washington Monument.

Saarinen's arch is what engineers call an inverted catenary. A catenary is the curve a chain takes when it is hung between two points.

Turn the hanging chain upside down: It becomes an arch.

From a structural standpoint, the catenary is the soundest arch of all. In some arches, pressure from the top can force the legs apart. In a catenary arch, the weight at the top presses down through

The Gateway Arch has been constructed to withstand earthquakes and high winds.

It is capable of swaying as much as 18 inches.

the arch's legs to be absorbed by the foundation.

The arch is often called the Gateway to the West or the Gateway Arch. As such, it reflects the spirit and determination of the western pioneers.

Eero Saarinen did not live to see the arch completed. He died in 1961, the same year construction work began on the arch.

In the first phase, massive concrete foundations were poured for each leg of the arch. The foundations were sunk 60 feet below the ground and 30 feet into the bedrock.

Each leg of the arch is three-sided and constructed of double walls of steel. The outer wall is sparkling stainless steel. The inner wall is tough carbon steel. Workers assembled the arch out of 142 steel sections. Some sections weighed as much as 50 tons.

Cranes operating from ground level lifted the first five sections for each leg into place one by one. Then a pair of creeper cranes took over. The creeper cranes, riding on tracks mounted on the completed portions of each leg, hoisted the remaining steel sections into position. Workers then bolted the sections together.

To strengthen the arch, workers filled the space between the steel walls of each section with concrete up to the 300-foot level. Beyond that point, steel-stiffening rods were installed.

A critical moment arrived late in October 1965 as the arch neared completion. Workers prepared to put the final section into place at the very top of the structure. About ten thousand people gathered on the riverbank near the arch to watch.

ON VIEW

The Gateway Arch is a stunning monument and historic landmark. At the highest point of the arch, there's an observation deck for visitors. A unique transportation system delivers visitors to the top.

At the visitors' center directly below the arch, passengers board a five-seat capsule that hoists them to the observation deck. It's a five-minute trip. The capsule operates like a Ferris wheel car, so passengers are always in a level position. Eight capsules operate in each leg of the arch.

The observation platform's sixteen plateglass windows provide views of 30 miles to the east and west on a clear day. There's room for as many as two hundred people at a time.

In case of a breakdown in the operation of a capsule, there are stairways in each leg. Hope that nothing goes wrong, though, because going down takes 1,076 steps.

About three million people visit the Gateway Arch each year. One million of these take the ride to the arch's observation deck.

The lobby visitors' center also offers a museum. Through films and exhibits, it tells the story of the nation's westward expansion.

The Gateway Arch is the tallest national monument of its type—75 feet taller than the Washington Monument, 325 feet taller than the Statue of Liberty.

After a spreader jack had forced apart the gap between the two legs, the final triangular steel section was eased into the opening, bolted, and then welded into place. Construction of the arch took four years.

The final steel section was 8 feet in width. But the sun's heat had expanded the steel in the arch's legs. As a result, the opening between the legs meant to receive the final section was only 2½ feet wide.

To make it wider, workers installed a spreader jack across the gap. By applying 450 tons of hydraulic force, the jack slowly pried open the space. As the crowd below cheered, a creeper crane lowered the

Before construction began, engineers forecast that as many as

thirteen workers might lose their lives on the project. Thanks to strict

safety rules, not one worker died.

final section into place.

The Gateway Arch can be seen for 30 miles. The Mississippi River flows past its base. Close by is the stately iron-domed old courthouse building, which dates from 1839. Once a landmark for steamboat captains, the courthouse now serves as the memorial's headquarters and museum. Soaring riverfront towers and a huge sports stadium, home to St. Louis's professional sports teams, now stand where once there were barren parking lots and unsightly rubble. A huge convention center lies just to the north.

Architectural critics agree that the Gateway Arch was Eero Saarinen's great success. He designed many notable buildings during his lifetime. They include the General Motors Technical Center in Warren, Michigan; the main terminal of Dulles International Airport near Washington, D.C.; and the futuristic TWA Terminal at New York City's John F. Kennedy International Airport, which looks like a bird in flight.

But it is his Gateway Arch that is often cited as Saarinen's outstanding achievement. In terms of its form and what it stands for, it is simply perfect.

The observation platform at the top of the arch can accommodate as many as 200 people at a time. Visitors get a panoramic view of the St. Louis riverfront, which includes a cobblestone pier with boats docked between its historic bridges.

Nine hundred tons of stainless steel were used in building the Gateway Arch. That's more stainless steel than was used in any other construction project ever.

DESIGN LINKS

Sightseers looking down from the Gateway Arch's observation deck can't help but notice the four nearby bridges that span the Mississippi River, linking St. Louis and East St. Louis. The arch makes use of engineering concepts reflected in two of these bridges. The Eads Bridge stands at the northern edge of the Jefferson National Expansion Memorial site. The upper and lower ribs of the bridge's four arches are fabricated of steel. This marked the first use of steel in an American bridge. The Gateway Arch echoes the Eads Bridge in both its use of steel and the arch concept. The Poplar Street Bridge, at the southern boundary of the memorial, represents another notable feat of engineering. It is the largest bridge in St. Louis, and it is the first American bridge of its size whose sections of steel plate were welded together. Welding was also used to join the triangular steel sections of the Gateway Arch.

101

What is the tallest building in the world? Chicago's Sears Tower, at 1,450 feet, once held that title. But in the years since the Sears Tower was completed in 1974, several taller skyscrapers have been built in Asian cities.

The matter of which building is the world's tallest is in dispute, however. Two 257-foot antenna towers have been erected on the roof of the Sears Building. They bring the building's total height to 1,707 feet. Those antennas, some say, enable the Sears Tower to still hold the "world's tallest" title.

There is one statement that no one questions: The Sears Tower is the tallest building in the United States and all of North America.

There's also agreement that Chicago is the right location for the Sears Tower. That's because the city of Chicago has had a long and very close connection with tall buildings.

It was in Chicago that the system of using an interior metal frame to support the floors and walls of tall buildings was developed. The ten-story Home Insurance Building, constructed in Chicago from 1884 to 1885, was the first building to utilize that principle. It is the ancestor of today's glass-and-steel skyscrapers.

Planning for the Sears Tower began in the late 1960s. At the time, Sears, Roebuck and Company, the nation's largest company selling consumer goods, occupied offices and warehouses on Chicago's West Side. But the buildings were old, and the company wanted more space.

After a year of searching, Sears found a suitable site in the West Loop section of Chicago. The property happened to be only a short distance from where the Home Insurance Building once stood.

Once the land had been purchased, architects and engineers began thinking about the building's design. One firm suggested building a tall, lean, four-sided tower, with the sides all equal in width. Engineers call this squared-tube construction. This style of building resembles a spaghetti box standing on one end.

Buildings of squared-tube design had been built before, but engineers for the Sears Tower took the concept

SEARS TOWER

LOCATION: Chicago, IL

TOTAL COST: $175 million ▪ CONSTRUCTION DATES: 1971–1974

HEIGHT: 1,450 feet (110 stories)

PLUMBERS' PROBLEM

Plumbers working to install the piping and fixtures important for supplying water in the Sears Tower were faced with many tough challenges.

How, for instance, in a building that stretches skyward for more than a quarter of a mile, do you get water to the upper floors when the city system provides water pressure that is reliable to only the first four or five floors?

The answer involves high-pressure pumps and a series of water-storage tanks. At the Sears Tower, plumbers installed tanks on the 31st, 64th, and 88th floors, and at rooftop level.

Powerful pumps drive water from the city system up into the tanks. The water then drains down from the tanks to the faucets and other fixtures on the floors below. Getting waste water down from the upper floors is easier. Gravity does the work.

The system is not trouble free, however. When water falls straight down through a pipe, the air below gets in the way. These air pockets cause turbulence, which disrupts the water's flow. Plumbers install small openings at intervals in the main pipe to allow the air to escape. To plumbers, this problem is known as the glug effect.

one step further. Instead of merely having one four-sided tube, they decided to have nine of them. They would bundle the nine into one cluster—three on each side, one in the center. Each tube would share walls with its neighbors.

Not all of the tubes would rise to the same height, however. Beginning at the 49th floor, some of the outer tubes would be topped off. Only two of the nine tubes would reach the building's full height.

In June 1971, a groundbreaking ceremony at the building site signaled the beginning of construction work. The building went up fast. Long steel derricks attached to each side of the building, called creeper derricks, hoisted massive sections of interlocking steel girders into place to form the tube walls. The derricks had a range of only four stories. Once construction was completed on one four-story section, the derricks were lifted and reinstalled at the next higher level.

As the building rose, workers applied fireproofing to the structural steel. They laid the floors and put on the exterior walls. They mounted black aluminum panels onto the outer surface of the walls and installed bronze-tinted windows. The building shot up at the rate of two stories per week.

On May 3, 1973, a creeper derrick lifted the final steel section into place. Workers held a "topping out" celebration. Other crews were still at work, finishing the building's interior. When completed in 1974, the Sears Tower took over as the tallest building in North America. The Twin Towers of the World Trade Center in New York had previously held the title.

In 1989, Sears sold its Tower. The company moved its employees to

Some floors in the Sears Tower offer 50,000 square feet of open space, which makes each of them almost big enough to hold three football fields.

Hoffman Estates, Illinois, a Chicago suburb, in 1995. Other companies moved in to occupy the former headquarters building, which kept the Sears Tower name.

The title of the nation's tallest building is not as desirable as it once was. The terrorist attacks that destroyed the World Trade Center's Twin Towers on September 11, 2001, changed the way many people think about supertall buildings.

To increase security, street-level barricades at the building's entrances are now part of the Sears Tower scene. Employees must show identification at security checkpoints to get to their offices.

On May 3, 2003, Chicagoans celebrated the thirtieth anniversary of the date on which the building was topped out. They applauded the fact that the Sears Tower serves as a workplace for ten thousand people each day and is visited by more than one million tourists a year. They saluted the building not only as one of the nation's most notable landmarks but also one of the great engineering achievements of the twentieth century.

Once the steel frame was up, fireproofing (the band of white in this photograph) was applied, and then the exterior walls were installed.

Operating from the Tower's roof, robotic window washers clean the building's black aluminum outer surface and its more than 16,000 windows.

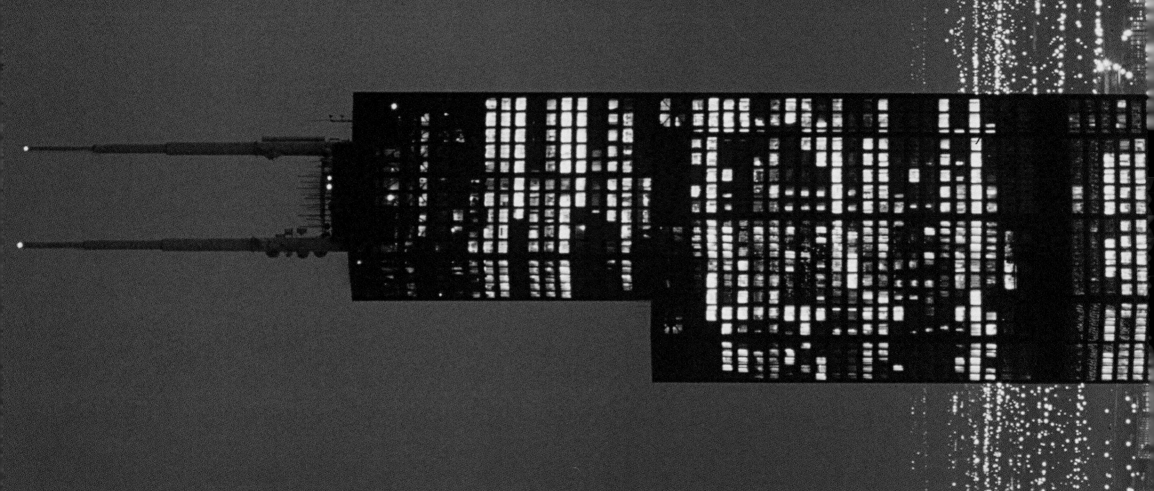

EVER HIGHER

The word *skyscraper* was first used around 1885, when tall buildings were starting to rise in Chicago and New York City. But the desire to build towering structures goes back many centuries. During the Middle Ages, castles and fortresses boasted tall, thick-walled towers of heavy stone. Soaring cathedrals, with their arched, stone frames, were the tall buildings of the Gothic era. Modern times brought steel-frame construction and the elevator, making it possible to build to daring heights. But as buildings became taller, engineers faced a problem practically unknown to castle and cathedral builders—the wind. Strong winds put enormous stress on the upper floors of tall buildings. The bundled tube design of the Sears Tower makes the problem less severe. The high floors required fewer tubes making them more flexible. Slip joints installed within the building's walls also help. As the wind hits the Sears Tower, the walls actually sway a little.

107

MEGAPROJECTS
1990—Present

T he 1900s are called the American Century. And no wonder. As the century drew to a close, the United States had no rival in terms of its worldwide influence. Its most powerful opponent for almost half of the century, the Soviet Union, had collapsed. America was the world's one and only superpower.

Several construction projects expressed the nation's wealth and power. These carried price tags, not in the millions but in the billions. These are megaprojects—extremely large; huge, in fact.

Megaprojects are seen as practical solutions to massive problems. They are public works projects, meaning they are paid for largely by federal and state governments and are meant for public use.

Often these huge projects benefit from new types of construction techniques and equipment. The mole—a monstrous, robotlike tunneling machine—is one. It normally takes a week of drilling and blasting for a forty- or fifty-man construction crew to tunnel 100 feet through hard rock. The mole advances that far in a single day.

Megaprojects include highways, mass-transit systems, water-supply systems, airports, convention centers, and sports stadiums. They are common to big cities.

Boston's Central Artery/Tunnel project is a megaproject. Completed in 2005 after more than a decade of work, it is the most complex highway project in American history. It had a megasize price tag, too. More than $14 billion was poured into the project.

In New York City, tunnel diggers working nearly 500 feet beneath the streets' surfaces are scooping out a 60-mile-long passage through hard rock that will deliver water to the city from upstate lakes and reservoirs. Although the tunnel is desperately needed, it won't be completed until 2020. The cost: $6 billion.

Denver International Airport, which began operation in 1993, is another megaproject. Called "the first airport of the twenty-first century," it is enormous—twice the size of Manhattan Island, in fact. That's mega, all right.

Chicago and Los Angeles have expanded and modernized their airports. In Chicago, the work cost $6 billion; in Los Angeles, $12 billion.

The terrorist attacks of September 11, 2001, jolted the nation's superpower status. New York City moved quickly to recover. Within months after the attack, the city announced plans to redevelop the site where the World Trade Center's Twin Towers once stood. Architects have proposed sky-high buildings, a memorial to the victims, a mass-transit complex, new streets, and a park. It's a true megaproject.

For well over a decade, the digging, bulldozing, backhoeing, and pile driving never stopped. Neighborhoods became war zones. People grumbled about the noise and dirt.

Traffic was snarled almost everywhere. Highway shutdowns were common. Off-ramps became on-ramps; exits disappeared overnight. Pedestrians struggled with makeshift sidewalks and muddy shoes.

"Boston is a nightmare," said a city visitor.

It was the most complex and expensive construction project ever undertaken by an American city. It was Boston's Central Artery/ Tunnel Project, or what everyone called the Big Dig.

The Big Dig involved several major elements. First, the Central Artery, an old and decaying elevated highway that cut through the heart of the city, was to be replaced by a state-of-the-art underground expressway.

The Big Dig project also included building a four-lane tunnel under Boston Harbor and a ten-lane bridge of unusual design over the Charles River.

In addition, the decaying water, sewer, gas, electrical, telephone, and steam lines running underneath the city's streets had to be dug up and replaced.

Engineers compared the Big Dig to the Panama Canal and other great construction projects of the past. But the Big Dig presented its own set of tough challenges. Engineers had to figure out how to install the new tunnels, bridges, and expressways and connect them to existing highways and streets. They had to do all of these things without shutting down the city.

Boston's problems with moving people and vehicles go back more than a century. That's mostly because Boston is built on a peninsula. Because there is water on three sides, there is little space to expand.

Bostonians lopped off the tops of hills and used the soil to create more land, but it was never enough. The waves of immigrants who flooded the city during the 19th century added to the problem.

CENTRAL ARTERY/ TUNNEL PROJECT

LOCATION: Boston, MA

TOTAL COST: $14.6 billion

CONSTRUCTION DATES: 1991–2005

When the automobile age arrived in the early 1900s, things got even worse. Cars were laughable on Boston's narrow, crooked streets.

City planners built highways and tunnels to carry traffic through and around the city. The Central Artery, an elevated highway that knifed through the oldest part of Boston, was one of the most important.

During construction of the Central Artery project, traffic jams were common. Above, Boston commuters seeking to enter the city are backed up along I-93 on a Monday morning in June 1999.

underwater, was the answer.

Work got underway late in 1991 when tugboats eased an oversize construction barge into Boston Harbor. Riding the barge was the Super Scoop, one of the world's largest seagoing dredges. It began taking SUV-size bites of muck from the harbor bottom.

During the next two years, the Super Scoop worked its way from one side of the harbor to the other, creating a mammoth trench, 50 feet deep and three-quarters of a mile long. The trench was the first step in constructing a four-lane tunnel beneath the harbor. By connecting two busy highways, the tunnel would prevent serious traffic bottlenecks, especially during rush hour.

The Central Artery opened in 1959. Bostonians quickly realized that it was a mistake. It divided downtown Boston and the city's North End from the waterfront. It brought dirt and noise to the center of the city. Unable to handle the huge number of cars using it, the Central Artery became a long stop-and-go traffic jam.

A new highway, partly underground and partly

The Central Artery/Tunnel Project used 3.8 million cubic yards of concrete.

That's enough concrete to build a sidewalk 3 feet wide and

3 inches deep around the world at the equator.

As the Super Scoop gnawed its way across Boston Harbor, a Baltimore, Maryland, shipyard was busy building the twelve steel sections that were to form the tunnel.

Each tunnel section was made up of a pair of huge steel tubes meant to carry two lanes of traffic. Each tube was about the size of a football field—320 feet long and 80 feet wide. Tugboats towing giant barges hauled the sections north along the Atlantic Coast to Boston.

One by one, towering cranes gently lowered the tunnel sections into the harbor trench. Once these were in place, workers removed the steel walls at the tube ends to form the tunnel.

The tunnel opened for traffic on December 15, 1995. It is named for Ted Williams of the Boston Red Sox, one of baseball's all-time greats.

As the Ted Williams Tunnel was being put together, another army of workers had begun building the underground tunnel and expressway that would replace the elevated highway known as the Central Artery.

To form the tunnel walls, workers first dug a series of deep trenches below and on either side of the Central Artery. As soon as the soil was removed from a trench, it was replaced by a mixture of powdered clay and water that looked like cake batter. Called slurry, the mixture held up the walls of the trench and prevented water from seeping in.

Workers then piped concrete through the slurry into the bottom of the trench. As the concrete flowed, the slurry rose to the top to be skimmed off. Workers continued to fill the trench with concrete until there was no slurry left. When the concrete hardened, it formed a tunnel wall.

RARE FIND

Some Bostonians of colonial times enjoyed bowling. We know this because archaeologists digging into the remains of an outhouse—that is, a privy or toilet—in Boston's North End found a small rounded object made of oak. It was almost five inches in diameter.

"The object turned out to be a bowling ball," says Dr. Ann-Eliza H. Lewis, archaeological collections manager for the Massachusetts Historical Society. Called a bowle, it was used in lawn bowling, not bowling at pins.

"You rolled your bowle over the grass toward a smaller ball known as a jack," says Dr. Lewis. "The idea was to get your bowle as close as possible to the jack."

Dr. Lewis and the other archaeologists believe that the bowle dates to the 1670s. Says Dr. Lewis, "That makes it the oldest known example of a bowling ball in North America."

The North End privy site was filled with trash and sealed with clay. It yielded fragments of glass and dishware, and animal bones from cows and pigs. There was also evidence of imported herbs, such as coriander, revealing that these Bostonians liked to spice up their food.

Big Dig engineers provided soundproof windows and soundproof curtains for homeowners living close to construction sites. These reduced the amount of noise penetrating a house.

When the tunnel walls were completed, workers began digging out the soil in between them. They placed heavy steel girders from one wall to the other to form a roof for the tunnel. Thick layers of concrete were laid on top of the steel.

The concrete and steel that roofed the tunnel supported the old elevated highway. Workers could begin construction of the new underground expressway without interrupting the flow of traffic above.

Today, the elevated Central Artery is gone. In its place is an array of new parks and office buildings. Beneath these, traffic moves briskly through the underground tunnel, unseen and unheard.

If the Big Dig has a symbol, it is the Leonard P.

A concrete slab is lowered into place to form a roadway section of what had been called the most expensive highway project in the nation's history.

Zakim Bunker Hill Bridge, built to replace an old and crumbling crossing. A stunning landmark, the Zakim Bridge spans the Charles River to link Boston with the part of the city known as Charlestown.

The Zakim Bridge is a suspension bridge. But it is wholly unlike other suspension bridges, such as the Golden Gate Bridge in San Francisco or Brooklyn Bridge in New York City.

The Zakim Bridge has a pair of tall towers, each of which takes the shape of an upside-down Y. They're unusual because they're asymmetrical (different heights). The south tower is 295 feet in height; the north tower, 35 feet taller. Both reach deep down into

During construction, a Boston ice-cream company served Big Dig sundaes.

For $4.99, it offered four scoops of Oreo cookie ice cream, crumbled Oreo cookies,

walnuts, hot fudge, peanut butter ice cream, and whipped cream.

the bedrock far beneath the river.

Most suspension bridges have two or four cables. The Zakim Bridge is much different. It has a network of 116 cables, or cable stays, that lead from the tops of the towers to support the roadway. The cables give the bridge a delicate, spidery look.

Each set of cable stays is placed at a different distance from the towers. The cable stays that are anchored farthest from the towers have the most work to do. They hold up the center of the bridge's main span.

The Zakim Bridge fully opened to traffic in 2003. Its ten lanes of roadway make it the widest cable-stayed bridge in the world.

Opened to traffic in 2003, the Leonard P. Zakim Bunker Hill Bridge uses both steel and concrete in the frame, which makes it the only "hybrid" cable-stayed bridge in the United States.

The bridge was named for Leonard P. Zakim, a noted Boston civil rights activist who spent much of his life fighting bigotry and hatred. The bridge also honors those men who fought in the Battle of Bunker Hill, which took place in Charlestown in 1775 during the Revolutionary War.

The new bridges and tunnels and the underground expressway have helped transform Boston. Traffic moves more smoothly. Acres of open space have been created. The city's waterfront neighborhoods and historic North End have been reconnected. The Big Dig has made Boston a better place to live and work.

When workers used dynamite to blast underwater rock formations, they were careful not to harm unwary fish. They used sonar equipment aboard an old lobster boat to send out a loud warning sound that startled the fish and caused them to flee before the blast went off.

City Tunnel No. 3 is a damp, dimly lit eerie place nearly 600 feet below the streets of New York City.

About forty tunnel diggers, known as sandhogs, work in Tunnel No. 3. They wear boots, steel helmets, and yellow slickers. With jumbo drills and dynamite, they are carving out the Manhattan section of a tunnel that will stretch 60 miles to huge reservoirs far north of the city. When completed in 2020, the tunnel will deliver the 1.3 billion gallons of water that New York City's eight million residents use every day.

The city now gets its water through two tunnels that have been in use since the early 1900s. City officials worry about those tunnels because they and the valves that control them have become battered by years of use. But engineers are unwilling to shut down the tunnels, stopping the water's flow, and make repairs. They're afraid the tunnels might collapse if they were to do so.

That could spell real disaster for the city. "If one of those tunnels goes, this city will be completely shut down," Jimmy Ryan, the tunnel diggers' foreman, told *The New Yorker*. "In some places there won't be water for anything. Hospitals. Drinking. Fires. It would make September eleventh look like nothing."

That's why New York City has an urgent need for Tunnel No. 3. It will allow engineers to temporarily stop the passage of water in the other two tunnels. Then they can be inspected and put in good condition again without interrupting the city's water supply.

City Tunnel No. 3 is a very expensive project. It is going to cost about $6 billion. And for good reason. It has been called "the greatest nondefense construction project in the history of Western civilization."

City Tunnel No. 3 has also proven very costly in terms of human lives. Some twenty-four people have died since tunnel construction started in 1970.

Since its earliest days, New York City has struggled

LOCATION: From Hillview Reservoir, Westchester County, NY, to New York City

TOTAL COST: $6 billion

CONSTRUCTION DATES: 1970–2020

UNDERGROUND MEN

Tunnel diggers are known as sandhogs. The name was first given to the men who dug out the soft earth for the foundations of the Brooklyn Bridge's towers in the 1870s.

After a strike in 1872, their weekly pay increased from $2.25 to $2.75 a week. It is much different today. Sandhogs are among the best paid construction workers. They can earn more than $100,000 a year.

The work sandhogs do is tough and very dangerous. Silicosis, an often fatal lung disease that results from breathing in rock dust, is a constant threat. Sandhogs wear face masks to protect themselves against silicosis.

Silicosis is only one of the perils that New York City sandhogs face. Some have been crushed by falling rock during cave-ins. Others have died in explosions. One man fell from the top of the tunnel-boring machine and fractured his skull. A hoisting machine fell down a shaft and killed another.

"We always lose someone on a job, no matter how many precautions we take," Richard Fitzsimmons, Sr., a union leader, told the *New York Times*. "That's the way it is."

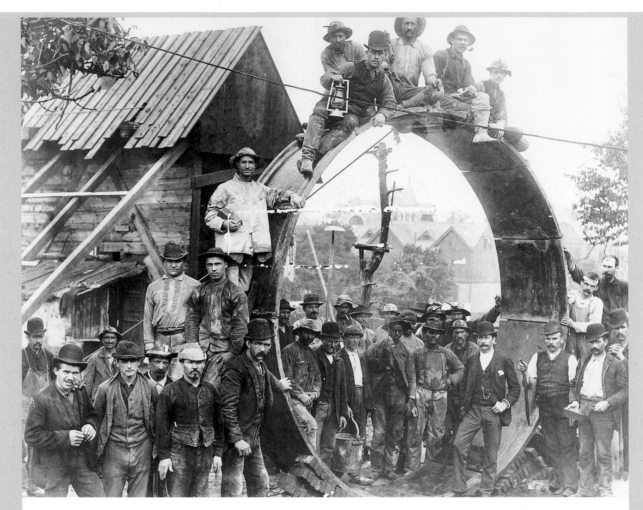

In 1885, work began on what was called the New Croton Aqueduct to supply water to New York City. Here, some of the construction workers pose with a steel tunnel section.

to get the water it needs. The first colonists depended on ponds, streams, and freshwater wells. But as the population increased, the purity of the city's water kept getting worse. During the 1830s, New York City suffered

New Yorkers use about a billion gallons of water daily. A billion 1-gallon plastic containers would stretch around the world at the equator more than five times.

from yellow fever, typhoid fever, and other diseases caused by poor water quality.

City officials then began to reach out beyond the city for water. By 1842, the city had dammed the Croton River in Westchester County north of the city and had started using the collected water as its chief supply source.

Over the next century, as the demand continued to climb, the city had to look farther and farther away for water. Today, the Catskill Mountains, more than 100 miles to the north, and the Delaware River Basin, west of the Catskills, supply 90 percent of New York City's clean water.

Tunnels and aqueducts (water-carrying systems covered with stone, brick, or concrete) carry the water to reservoirs for storage. Water goes into City Tunnels

The 20-foot rotating blade of the 450-ton boring machine known as the mole cut this cylinder-shaped passage through the hard rock that lies some 600 feet below the streets of New York City.

Nos. 1 and 2 from the reservoirs before being piped into homes, offices, and apartment buildings.

In some places, Tunnel No. 3 is up to 24 feet in diameter. That makes it big enough to carry a freight train. The tunnel air is warm and heavy with dust. Light comes from electric bulbs that hang down from wires clamped to the black-rock tunnel walls.

Working in ankle-deep muddy water, sandhogs bore 10-foot-deep holes into the tunnel face. They shoot bursts of air and water into the holes to clean them out. Then they pack the holes with sticks of dynamite, which are connected by wires to a detonator at street level.

Before blasting, a metal elevator that looks like a cage hoists the sandhogs almost sixty stories to the surface. When a foreman gives the signal, a worker

New York City's sandhogs got started as an organized group on May 8, 1872.

That's the day 200 laborers, many of them Irish immigrants, went on strike

during the digging of the foundations of the Brooklyn Bridge.

sets off the charge. Its loud roar startles unsuspecting pedestrians. The sidewalk trembles, and the chain-link fence around the street-level construction site rattles and shakes.

"All right!" the foreman yells. The sandhogs descend by elevator into the tunnel to resume drilling and blasting.

In another section of the tunnel, a 230-ton tunnel-boring machine, or mole, has replaced drilling and blasting. The mole is huge, stretching to the length of several school buses inside the tunnel. Its powerful steel arms grip the tunnel walls and push the machine through muddy water to the rock face.

The mole's huge circular head is fitted with twenty-seven big cutters, each weighing 320 pounds. When pressed into the tunnel's rock face, the cutters spin furiously, biting into the rock. The racket blots out all other sound. The mole hacks out as much as 100 feet of rock a day.

Excavated rock is pulverized, then hauled by rail to a shaft where the rubble is hoisted to the surface. Cables for delivering power and ducts bringing in clean air line the tunnel walls.

About half of New York City's water supply travels through the Delaware Aqueduct,

which is 85 miles long and listed in *The Guinness Book of World Records* as

the longest water-supply tunnel in the world.

During his term as mayor of New York City, Michael Bloomberg put on rubber boots and a yellow slicker and visited the tunnel work site. He sloshed through the mud to chat with the sandhogs.

While visiting, the mayor noted the city's pressing need for Tunnel No. 3. He said it would provide extra layers of security for the city by allowing engineers to shut down the two aging tunnels so necessary repairs could be made.

But tunnel construction is subject to delays. Rising costs have halted work from time to time. Even longer delays have been caused by people who protest the drilling of tunnel shafts in their neighborhoods. They say the work brings dirt and noise.

"It would be a very big problem for the city if one of those two tunnels were to collapse in any one portion," Mayor Bloomberg told reporters. "It could take up to a year to dig down, and repair it, and get it back in service.

"We can live without a lot of things," the mayor said. "Water is not one of them."

The tunnel conveyer system delivers pulverized rock to the surface, forming a big pyramid-shaped pile.

Sandhogs have created a great maze beneath New York City, including

more than 400 miles of subway tunnels, 6,000 miles of sewers,

and thousands of miles of gas mains.

FOR FURTHER READING

Books

Stephen E. Ambrose. *Nothing Like It in the World: The Men Who Built the Transcontinental Railroad, 1863–1869*. New York: Simon & Schuster, 2000.

Robert F. Arteaga. *The Building of the Arch*. St. Louis: Jefferson National Parks Association, 2002.

Donald R. Kennon, editor. *The United States Capitol: Designing and Decorating a National Icon*. Athens: Ohio University Press, 2000.

Elizabeth Mann. *Hoover Dam: The Story of Hard Times, Tough People, and the Taming of a Wild River*. New York: Mikaya Press, 2001.

Andy Olenick and Richard O. Reisem. *Erie Canal Legacy: Architectural Treasures of the Empire State*. Rochester: Landmark Society of Western New York, 2000.

Kathy Pelta. *Bridging the Golden Gate*. Minneapolis: Lerner Publications, 1987.

Jay Pridmore. *Sears Tower: A Building Book from the Chicago Architecture Foundation*. San Francisco: Pomegranate, 2002.

Mary J. Shapiro. *A Picture History of the Brooklyn Bridge*. New York: Dover Publications, 1983.

John Tauranac. *The Empire State Building: The Making of a Landmark*. New York: St. Martin's, 1995.

Peter Vanderwarker. *The Big Dig: Reshaping an American City*. Boston: Little, Brown, 2001.

John van der Zee. *The Gate: The True Story of the Design and Construction of the Golden Gate Bridge*. New York: Simon & Schuster, 1987.

Magazine articles

"Fort Peck—A Half Century and Holding." *District News*, Omaha District, Corps of Engineers, 50th Anniversary Commemorative Issue, Vol. 11, No. 2, Summer 1987.

David Grann. "City of Water." *The New Yorker* (September 1, 2003): 88–103.

WEB SITES

IN GENERAL www.pbs.org/wgbh/buildingbig/index.html

ERIE CANAL

http://www.epodunk.com/routes/erie-canal/index.html#

http://www.eriecanal.org/

HOOSAC TUNNEL

http://www.intac.com/~jsumberg/hoosac.htm

UNITED STATES CAPITOL

http://www.aoc.gov/cc/cc_overview.htm

BROOKLYN BRIDGE

http://www.endex.com/gf/buildings/bbridge/bbridgefacts.htm

FLATIRON BUILDING

http://www.greatbuildings.com/buildings/Flatiron_
Building.html

TRANSCONTINENTAL RAILROAD

http://memory.loc.gov/ammem/gmdhtml/rrhtml/
rrintro.html#TR

EMPIRE STATE BUILDING

http://www.fiddlersgreen.net/buildings/new-
england/empire-state/info/info.htm

FORT PECK DAM

http://www.nwo.usace.army.mil/html/Lake_Proj/fortpeck/
history.html

HOOVER DAM

http://www.usbr.gov/lc/hooverdam/History/

http://www.usbr.gov/lc/hooverdam/History/essays/index.html

GOLDEN GATE BRIDGE

http://utut.essortment.com/historygoldeng_refh.htm

http://www.sfmuseum.org/hist9/mcgloin.html

CASCADE TUNNEL

http://mikes.railhistory.railfan.net/r004.html

U.S. INTERSTATE HIGHWAY SYSTEM

http://www.fhwa.dot.gov/programadmin/interstate.html

CHESAPEAKE BAY BRIDGE-TUNNEL

www.cbbt.com/facts.html

JEFFERSON NATIONAL EXPANSION MEMORIAL ARCH

http://www.nps.gov/jeff/arch.html

SEARS TOWER

http://www.searstower.org/home.html

CENTRAL ARTERY/TUNNEL PROJECT

http://www.bigdig.com

CITY TUNNEL NO. 3

http://www.nyc.gov/html/dep/html/news/3rdtunnel.html

INDEX

ACKNOWLEDGMENTS

A book as wide-ranging as this one, with sections explaining construction projects from the nation's earliest days to the present, requires contributions from a multitude of people. Some provided background information or photographs; others vetted chapters for accuracy. Special thanks are due to photo researcher Athena Angelos for her diligence and resourcefulness; Jennifer L. Rawlings, archivist, Jefferson National Expansion Memorial; Janet Parks and Lou di Gennaro, Avery Architectural and Fine Arts Library, Columbia University; Meg Ventrudo, Museum of American Financial History; Darrin J. McMurry, Corps of Engineers, Fort Peck, Montana; Dale E. Waterman, Western Gateway Heritage State Park, North Adams, Massachusetts; Gail Bailey and Gillian Jones, *North Adams Transcript*; Dennis Rahilly, Holly Sutherland, and Cynthia Monahan, Central Artery/Tunnel Project, Boston; Ann-Eliza H. Lewis, archaeological collections manager, Massachusetts Historical Commission; Robert B. Hitchins, archivist, Kirn Library, Norfolk, Virginia; Lorraine Smith and Paige B. Addison, Chesapeake Bay Bridge-Tunnel; Kimberly Ettinger, *Newport News Daily Press*; Aimee Marshall, Chicago Historical Society; Natalie Millner and Scott Foster, Department of Environmental Protection, New York City; Marcia Kees, New York State Office of Parks, Recreation, and Historic Preservation; Karen Cowan, Bureau of Reclamation; Richard Coleman and Allen Alden, Federal Highway Administration; Andy Kitzmann, Erie Canal Museum; Ken Cobb, Municipal Archives, City of New York; Daile Kaplan, Swann Galleries; James Levin, Studio 10, New York City; Bill Fitzgerald, Wide World Photos; and Jed M. Best.

Special thanks are also due to Elysa Jacobs, my editor at Scholastic, for originating this project, steering it through the approval process, and supervising editorial matters up until its final stages. Kate Waters, Ted Ashley, Brenda Murray, and Nancy Sabato skillfully directed operations in the book's last year of design and production. To all of them, I'm very grateful.

GEORGE SULLIVAN

PHOTO CREDITS

Library of Congress Cataloging-in-Publication Data
Sullivan, George, 1927– ▪ Built to last: Building America's amazing bridges, dams, tunnels,
and skyscrapers / George Sullivan ▪ 1. Civil engineering—United States History—Juvenile
literature. I. Title. ▪ TA23.S85 2005 ▪ 624'.0973—dc22 ▪ 2004060996

ISBN 0-439-51737-0

10 9 8 7 6 5 4 3 2 1   05 06 07 08 09

Printed in Singapore   46
First printing, October 2005

The text was set in 11-point Caecilia.
Book design by Nancy Sabato
Maps by Scholastic Inc./Jim McMahon

▪ ▪ ▪